Rastafari Women

RastafarI Women

Subordination in the Midst of Liberation Theology

Obiagele Lake
DEPARTMENT OF ANTHROPOLOGY
THE UNIVERSITY OF IOWA

CAROLINA ACADEMIC PRESS
Durham, North Carolina

Library of Congress Cataloging-in-Publication Data

Lake, Obiagele.
  RastafarI women : subordination in the midst of liberation theology /
Obiagele Lake.
      p.   cm.
  Includes bibliographical references and index.
  ISBN 0-89089-836-7 (pbk)
  1. Women in the Rastafari movement—Jamaica. 2. Jamaica—Religion.
I. Title.
BL2566.J25L34   1998
299'.676'082097292—dc21   98-11542
                                                               CIP

The cover photograph and photographs in Chapter 7 are by the author.

CAROLINA ACADEMIC PRESS
700 Kent Street
Durham, North Carolina 27701
Telephone (919) 489-7486
Fax (919) 493-5668
www.cap-press.com

Printed in the United States of America

To African Sisters the World Over

Contents

Tables and Figures

Acknowledgments

I extend my sincerest gratitude to all of the Rastafarian sisters who were so generous with their time and with their willingness to share parts of their lives with me. In particular, I am grateful to Maureen Rowe for her keen insights and to Sister Minnie allowing me to witness her indomitable spirit.

I am also grateful to Joann Quiñones-Podomo, my research assistant, for her diligent attention to all aspects of this tome during the crucial stages of this process. My sincerest thanks to my son, Jahmal, for his reading and critique of this work in its final stages.

RastafarI Women

Chapter 1

Rastafarian Women and the Global Struggle for Liberation

Women, since time immemorial, have been perceived as a threat by men in all parts of the globe. This threat is predicated on the possibility of women acting independently of men. Prior to the emergence of bureaucratic societies, women were kept in line by simple brute force. In contemporary societies physical force continues to play a large role in the domination of women as does their subordinate economic status compared to men. Moreover, women are systematically controlled by a panoply of ideas and values that deem them inferior to and, therefore, less valued than men. Ideology that deems women inferior is evident in print and electronic media, in music, in religious texts, and in everyday parlance. This cultural hegemony legitimates women's subordination in all parts of the world.

Men who have advocated for the liberation of African people in the African Diaspora are not exempt from sexist attitudes and behaviors toward African women. Rastafarians stand out as an example par excellence of this contradiction since they are viewed by many as being in the vanguard of revolutionary movements. Rastafarian men have dominated leadership positions within the organization and consider women to be secondary in all matters pertaining to RastafarI. This position, although anathema to the idea of freedom, is not surprising given the existence of global patriarchy and the entrenchment of sexism in Jamaica. Nevertheless, these uneven relations are significant as they point to men's propensity to exclusively struggle for *male* power—a focus that has historically pervaded all Diaspora African movements. Thus, my focus on Rastafarians is not to single them out as atypical, but to offer them as a microcosm that depicts African and Diaspora African female/male relations in general.

Jamaican Rastafarians constitute a socio-religious group that emerged out of a rebellious environment and a religious ethos of Ethiopianism (see Appendix A for Jamaican/Rastafarian Chronology). Their basic tenets include the belief in the divinity of Haile Selassie, the belief that *ganja* (marijuana) is a holy herb, and the conviction that the redemption of Diaspora Africans lies in their repatriation to Africa.

Since the inception of Rastafarianism in the 1930s, Rastas have protested against European colonial control over African descended people in

Jamaica. Freedom from colonial, capitalist hegemony and self-determination for African Diaspora people have constituted the cornerstones of their philosophy. As adamant as many Rastas are in these beliefs, they have not seen liberation as a right of women.

To say that Rastafarian women are subordinated to Rasta men is not tantamount to claiming that women are pawns, that they have no agency or influence, or that they have no personal power. Neither does the claim of women's subordination mean that they do not respect themselves or are not respected in certain ways by males in the organization. Women are respected if they maintain the rules that suppress them. Having said this, it is important to point out that on a case by case basis, there are Rastafarian women who are confident, active, and self-assertive. But, these women, who would probably not be servile to anyone, are in the minority.

Women's subordination is not a subtle notion, but one which is openly declared by Rastafarian women and men. Women's relegation to second class status is demonstrated in the minutia of everyday life with their menfolk where deference to men is the rule. Based on women's presumed inferiority, many believe that they must be brought into the organization by a man. Women are also considered polluted because of their capacity to menstruate and bear children. Most Rastas do not see these uneven relations as problematic, but the natural order of things as prescribed in the Christian Bible. Women's status is further denigrated by dress codes which conceal their bodies and symbolically shroud them in a veneer of feminine protection. Language which refers to women as "daughters" also diminishes women in relationship to men. In addition, reggae music, which has become a vehicle for the spread of RastafarI to almost all continents, acts as a fifth column in its derogation of women as sex objects and as dependents of men.

Rastafarian Women Literature

There is a plethora of literature that speaks to the evolution of RastafarI[1], (Chevannes 1990; Barrett 1988, 1977; Simpson 1985, 1956; Owens 1976) but very little of this body of work has lent space to a substantive discussion of Rastafarian women. As is true for other Diaspora African groups, RastafarI as an organization and as a discourse, has been articulated in male terms and in terms of male desires. This omission is primarily

---

1. RastafarI is a term frequently used by Rastafarians to connote the organization itself and the belief systems that Rastafarians embrace. I use the term in the same sense in this text.

due to the marginalized position that women have within Rasta organizations and the bias that researchers themselves have had in their approach to this group. More recently, a few women writers (Rowe 1985, Llalo 1981, and Waters 1985) have addressed issues related to the subordination of Rasta women. The purpose of this text, which is based on more than fourteen years of research among Jamaican Rastafarians, is to complement and broaden these works to include the nature and process of Rasta women's subordination and to suggest how it articulates with the marginalization of Jamaican (and Diaspora African) women as a whole. While other students of RastafarI have addressed dominant/subordinate relations, a holistic presentation of these issues which elaborates on male dominance and male privilege and ways that these institutions are played out in everyday life has not been fully explored.

The task of this work is to produce an exegesis of Rasta women that explicates the articulation between material and cultural power. Given the nature of literature that has been produced on this group, it is also important that I accomplish this in a way that does not glorify Rastafarians. This task is risky given the popular mystique regarding Rasta.[2]

---

2. Terisa Turner (1991:66–89) exceeds the limits of mystification by creating a totally fictionalized version of RastafarI, especially Rastafarian women, and labels it the "new Rastafari." Not only does she claim that Rastas and other women's groups are successfully militating against Structural Adjustment Programs and other international capitalist machines, she contends that "gender relations...are most obviously marked by women's economic autonomy....[A]bsent among the new Rasta women are those 'baby mothers' who, under threat of violence, must support financially and through the provision of domestic and sexual services, their children's fathers." While Rasta women may or may not be financially supporting their men, (which probably varies from case to case), 'baby mothers' continue to provide sexual and domestic services, sometimes under threat of violence that Turner pretends does not exist.

There are two important dangers (and thus the reason for even addressing this article) here. The first is that the wide popularity surrounding Rastafarians has allowed a number of scholars to become Rasta "experts" (without having done the work). Nowadays, presenting Rasta within the mystique of revolutionary change is a fad. Turner's research indicates an absence of empirical, in depth research in Jamaica and a misrepresentation of women's predicament in Africa and Jamaica (See Chapter 5 in this volume for substantiated data regarding the condition of women relative to men in Jamaica). For data on the predicament on women in various parts of Africa, see, e.g., Obbo (1980), Sigot, et al. (1995), Mbilinyi (1989:209–256), Brown 1989:257–278), McClendon (1995), and Parpart (1995); Another problem is that people of European descent have been writing and rewriting African people's history since forever. Because of their privileged position within academic circles, and on the printed page in general, their reconstruction and renaming (e.g., "new Rastafari") of African descended people and their struggles becomes paradigmatic in the minds of many.

With a few exceptions, the bulk of the literature mystifies Rastafarians as a revolutionary Black consciousness group that has encouraged other African communities to experience and express their African identities. While it is true that their influence on African Jamaicans was considerable during the 1960s, Rastafarian African consciousness has atrophied into musical rhythms and the consumption of *ganja*—aspects which have popularized the organization internationally. These popular dimensions have advanced the careers of individual Rastas and have provided entertainment around the world, but they have done little to advance the masses of African Jamaicans in concrete terms. Moreover, even their political ideology has become reduced to a movement for human peace and love, and one which is devoid of the racial imperative that typified the organization in the 1940s and 1950s. While "peace and love" are laudable in the abstract, the focus on these concepts at the expense of organizing for economic and political change is questionable.

The literature also abounds on the globalization of RastafarI which emphasizes the fascination of Japanese (Collinwood and Kusatsu, n.d), Australian, European, and Native American people (Trepper 1984:13–15,45) with reggae and *ganja*. Unfortunately, Rasta has been disseminated primarily through reggae music which, while adding to the breadth of the movement, has subtracted from the depth of Rastafarian values. Rasta groups who are, for example, European or Japanese, are not attracted to nor committed to an Afrocentric ideology, but to *ganja*, dreadlocks, and reggae which represent anti-establishment norms. Groups that have sprung up in various parts of the Diaspora (Gjerset 1994) also tend to embrace these symbols, but, by and large, do not incorporate the African centered ideology that was once characteristic of the organization.

Since the 1960s, social science disciplines have treated Rasta as a convenient topic of investigation—one which allows scholars to use Rasta rhetoric to create an image of revolutionary discourse without fully examining the difference between parlance and practice. This is especially important in terms of the predicament of Rastafarian women. For example, heretofore, there has been no work that elaborates on how the circumstances of Rasta women articulate with the sexist conditions in Jamaica (and the rest of the Diaspora) that spawned this male dominated dynamic. This

---

It would be comfortable for members of the dominant class to pretend that women of African descent and other oppressed people have liberated themselves when, in fact, they remain very much under the yoke of international racism and sexism fueled by the collusion of local and international elites.

book seeks to explicate these issues and to discuss ways in which many Rastafarian women in Jamaica have internalized their own oppression.

Another issue that makes this work risky is that male domination over women has been so long-standing, pervasive, and ubiquitous, that most people have accepted the inequity of male/female relations as natural. This perspective sets up extraordinary resistance to efforts that delineate women's oppression and ways that it can be combatted. Such resistance notwithstanding, this book attempts to situate Rasta women's subordination within a broader cultural, political, and economic framework where the marginalization of women is the rule.

Any treatise on women of African descent which falls within a feminist, or what I would prefer to call womanist (Walker 1983), framework draws the ire of many women and men of African descent. Racism is held up as *the* dragon to be slain and sexism is defined as secondary or non-existent (Terrelonge 1995:490–501). This ideology stems, in part, from the mythology that pre-colonial continental African societies were egalitarian and that Africans transported this social system during the trans-Atlantic voyage. When male transgressions against women are undeniable, they are attributed to European colonialism and capitalist development. Even though European hegemony has influenced all aspects of African life, it cannot be held up as the source of all evils. In pre-colonial Africa, lack of equal access to land, male violence against women, and female genital mutilation stand out as three of many indicators that point to women's derogated position. Another ploy which has worked to silence discussion of Diaspora African women's subordination is the claim of "cultural relativity".

Many scholars have spent a great deal of time discussing whether or not "western" (often meaning North American) women *should* critique Third World societies. This line of reasoning is, at best, shallow (in spite of the fact that those who propose it see themselves as quite liberal and sophisticated) since critique, in general, is a naturally occurring intellectual activity in all human beings. People constantly evaluate and critique others who are inside and outside of their own communities—not just from west to east, or north to south. Anthropologists then, who engage in such critiques and whose very interest is people, do so from a natural and a scholastic propensity. Moreover, to claim that cultural relativity is the question and the answer to everything leaves us all voiceless unless we are only in the business of *describing* cultures. My aim, as a woman of African American descent and as an anthropologist, entails a bit more. Primarily I seek to underscore the articulation between economic and personal dependence and to point to the connection between material, physical, and cultural power. In this regard, Rastafarian women are the focus of this essay not because they are an anomaly, but because, in palpable ways, they embody the sexist aspects of female/male relations globally.

Feminist Approaches—What is Missing?

The anthropological literature has contributed much to feminist theory (see e.g., Moore 1988; Rosaldo and Lamphere 1974). Unfortunately, anthropology has paid scant attention to the containment of women in the African Diaspora.[3] Nevertheless feminist theorists have proposed several basic paradigms with which we can view the dynamics of sexual[4] inequality. Some of the more salient perspectives include liberal, radical, socialist, post-modernist, and Black feminism.

Proponents of liberal feminism advocate working within the capitalist system in order to bring about an end to discrimination in jobs and education. This strategy is counterrevolutionary in so far as it fails to see that the very nature of "the system" creates and sustains uneven relations. Radical feminists have the same blind spot in proposing to work for the maintenance of the system. The difference between liberal and radical feminisms is that the latter would form autonomous female groups (no men allowed) in order to avoid the subordinate roles women usually assume in relationship to men.

Socialist feminists come close to attacking the problem at the source—economics. They suggest that the fundamental cause of sexism is the division of labor where women are categorically placed in inferior economic positions. While this observation is important, socialist proponents do not suggest viable strategies that would replace capitalism. If the tactics used by non-feminist socialists in America is any guide, then socialist strategies would be limited to increased militancy in labor unions while leaving the capitalist structure intact.

Post-modern feminists offer little to women in their struggle for equal access. The fundamental problem with anthropological post-modernist ideology is that it focuses on the trees and insists that the existence of the forest is a matter of opinion. This level of thinking may satisfy the intel-

3. Exceptions include the work by Faye Harrison (1988) who addresses important aspects of women's subordination in Jamaica and how their marginalization is a product of internal and external pressures. Lynn Bolles' (1996) empirical research in Jamaica regarding survival strategies of working class women in the late 1970s and the impact of IMF policies in the 1980s (Bolles 1983) has also filled an important gap in the literature.

4. I have intentionally avoided the term *gender* here (and will do so whenever possible throughout this text) since it has become misused and abused. The term is also used by various scholars to mean different things and as as spring board to join the women's bandwagon. As stated by Mohammed (1994:140n), "Gender is a much bandied about and overused word in scholarship at present, both internationally and in the Caribbean. Yet, in my view, the analytical capacity of this word means for many proponents and novices merely to 'add women and stir.'"

lectual needs of some academics, but, given its propensity to question the existence of any objective reality, it can do little to address the concrete structural problems inherent in racist/sexist dynamics relevant to the lives of African women. Post-modernist research, on the whole, has done more in advancing the careers of scholars than it has in addressing solutions to the problems of impoverished and oppressed peoples.

Contributions from Black feminists have been crucial in outlining the unique circumstances of women of African descent by calling attention to the interlocking features of class, sexism, and racism (Collins 1990; Giddings 1992:445). While these interlocking dimensions are oft repeated by other African American feminists, it is important to point out that not all scholars focus on the same aspects of sexist oppression. Terrelonge (1995:490–501) presents what I consider one of the most cogent examinations. She states that a feminist consciousness on the part of all people of African descent requires that women and men work together to address the social and economic ills that plague them. She also states that African Americans need to eschew the "societal definitions of appropriate sexual behaviors" (Ibid:497) which constrain the development of "individual talents." This, as well as reconditioning ourselves regarding restrictive ideas that define femininity and masculinity, would

> foster greater psychological well-being and thereby strengthen the interpersonal bonds that are constantly being eroded and loosened by the impact of interpersonal sexism.

Attention to these interpersonal and psychological aspects are important because it is at this level that we experience sexism in our daily lives. What is also missing from African American feminist analysis is a more thorough discussion of capitalist dynamics and ways in which it facilitates racist and sexist behaviors.

The penchant for men of African descent to strive for male power over and above Europeans or in collusion with European males, by definition leaves women out on the margins. African American men in past or contemporary history have not mounted a campaign to destroy the capitalist system, but to share power within the existing paradigm.

In this regard, I suggest that an entire new social and political structure is necessary in order for women and men to experience true freedom. More specifically, the liberation of women must occur along with the liberation of Jamaica as a whole. Following the work of Beckford (1988) bringing about this liberation within a plantation society would require "a high degree of co-ordination among Third World countries to make it difficult for [multinational] companies to play off one country against the other" (Ibid:222). This requires the integration of trans-national economies and the willingness to dismantle the present systems within those economies. Before any of this can happen people need to create a new vision of themselves.

> This creates self-confidence and sets the stage for head-on confrontation with the plantation system to destroy it and to create a new social order (Ibid:234).

This struggle for a liberated territory, of necessity, must be waged by women and men. Any other scenario would be tantamount to a replication of the old order.

Women's Containment within a Capitalist Political Economy

My own perspective cannot be neatly situated in any one of the feminisms outlined above, although it embraces some aspects of socialist and Black feminist thought. Certainly, to address capitalism head-on is a fundamental and initial step that must be taken. Capitalism as an institution is rarely specifically mentioned in women's organizations in Jamaica. Rastafarians, even though they are not actively organizing against this system, have at least recognized the necessity of articulating the central role of capitalism in the suppression of African people.

Nevertheless, the work of many Black feminists is significant since it underscores the interlocking dimensions of racism and sexism as they apply to all women of African descent. These insights notwithstanding, a paradigm that encompasses the range of sexualities that exist within the Diaspora African population is all but absent. Hammond (1997:181) avers that "[B]lack lesbian experience [must be] explored and historicized." To date, African American and Caribbean lesbians are producing one body of thought and other feminists are creating another. Hammond suggests that what is needed is

> a different level of engagement between black heterosexual and black lesbian women as the basis for the development of a black feminist praxis that articulates the ways in which invisibility, otherness, and stigma are produced and re-produced on black women's bodies. And ultimately my hope is that such an engagement will produce black feminist analyses which detail strategies for differently located black women to shape interventions that embody their separate and common interests and perspectives.

Indeed, the efforts by many Diaspora African women to throw off the image of a hypersexualized or deviant being precludes their attention to these issues.

In many Diaspora African communities homosexuals are branded with a label of *traitor*—a badge they feel they can ill afford given that they are alienated from other communities and would like to feel that they can find a safe place in their own. The tendency of people of African descent to actually and ideologically militate against homosexuality is very significant since an acceptance of same sex unions would entail a total restructuring of male/female norms. This is not to suggest that homosexuality is "the answer," but to emphasize that the acceptance of the lesbian alternative would at the same time require a serious questioning of male privilege and male supremacy.

Instead, what we have now is many Black feminists and other women spending more energy defending "Black manhood" than they do their own liberation. While it is not my intention to dismiss the oppression that both women and men of African descent experience, it is important to underscore the tendency of some women to identify "the-problem-of-the-Black-male" as more urgent than their own. This self-derogation plays into their very subordination.

My own vision of women's liberation encompasses a truly egalitarian society which, by definition, means that power and control belong in the hands of the people—women and men. I define power here as control over the means of production—those resources that are absolutely essential for survival. Women and men who value these ideals must be willing to struggle, violently if necessary, to obtain their rightful access to the fruits of the land. My thesis is that historically, men have abused power all over the world and that women have actively participated in their own oppression. Male dominance has been wielded by virtue of men's physical and material power and has been buttressed by religious and other cultural ideologies that sacralize power and privilege and the oppression and derogation of women.

Caribbean Responses to Male Domination

While the problems of all women in the Caribbean are not exactly the same—given differences in race, class, and sexual orientation—their subordination emanates from the same source: men's control over physical, material, and cultural resources. According to Mohammed (1994), Caribbean women have attempted to address their status in a number of ways. This attention to women's subordination has often taken the form of women's groups such as the *Concerned Women for Progress* in Trinidad and the *Committee of Women for Progress* in Jamaica which were tied to socialist organizations. Female and male scholars at the University of the West Indies (UWI) have also furthered research on women by establishing the Center for Gender and Development Studies.

Sistren is a non-government and non-academic organization that has waged battles on many fronts including making women aware of legal pro-

tections in terms of violence against them, presenting rural theater drama-
tizations for consciousness raising, and lobbying for the elimination of
derogatory media images of women, to name a few (Ford-Smith
1997:213–258).

Women's organizations abound in Jamaica, yet many women in these
groups reject the term "feminist" since 1) they equate it with North American feminist thought; and 2) the term conjures up anti-male images—both
of which are anathema in a phallocentric society like Jamaica. Unfortunately, feminism, in the minds of many people in and outside of Jamaica,
represents an "either/or" dichotomy and suggests to its adherents that one
must choose between being of African descent or being a woman (hooks
1984:27–41). This line of thinking has been fostered by men and internalized by women who fail to recognize the complexity of their identities
as African and female and that each and both are as important as being
African and male. To make the mental leap over this hurdle is to make
the leap out of mental slavery. It is not so important that more Jamaican
women adopt the term "feminist" as it is that they make the connection
between inequalities in the broader political and economic spheres of society with inequalities in their everyday interactions with men.

Many women outside of the academy have cast a disparaging glance
at women in patriarchal institutions since the latter are perceived as working in and for the very institutions that oppress them. Mohammed
(1994:140) counters that

> Some feminists have argued...that the objective of entering the halls of
> the academy is to create change by becoming part of the institution and pos-
> ing challenges from within. This division between activism and the acad-
> emy is at best a spurious one as the development of women's studies/gen-
> der studies provides an institutional memory for the feminist movement.

Mohammed further suggests that people working within the academy
can provide theoretical direction to the feminist movement.

We must also recognize that each one of us is our own leader and that
academics have as much to learn from sisters outside of the hallowed
halls as the other way around. Our quest then should not be the formu-
lation of prescriptions for other women, but to make the journey from the
ivory tower to the *yard* in order to, as Rastas say, "reason" together. In
this way, we need not fear replicating the patriarchal hierarchy
(Mohammed 1994:141) that we are trying to dismantle.

Lest we repeat W. E. B. DuBois' talented tenth approach, we in academia need to find ways to communicate with women outside of academia.
We must do so in such a way that allows us to listen to their experiences.
This must take place in an environment where leadership is shared. Moreover, if academics are serious about helping to create a society where all

citizens are truly free, then our struggle is to work so that we can look forward to a day when organizations based on gender are longer necessary.

That is, if women (and men) are serious about creating an egalitarian society, then we must struggle to the point where "gender" studies are no longer needed. A key question in this regard is whether "gender," like race, is just another way for middle class and elite scholars to accumulate fame and money or is it something we are committed to for women's benefit and for humanity as a whole? Difficult questions.

In this regard, one important task that I set for myself is to reveal the complexity of women's oppression in order to broaden the general and the anthropological literature. This involves delineating ways in which local and international capitalism superexploits women. In addition to looking at macro-economic structures, it is essential to examine ways that women are dominated at everyday levels and how they are conditioned at very young ages to defer to males. This domination by males of African descent is, in part, a legacy of male/female inequalities in Africa. That is, the domination of Rasta women (and by implication Caribbean and all women) is not only an artifact of racial oppression, but a continuation of pre-colonial African hierarchical systems which routinely and systematically oppressed (and continue to oppress) women. Rastafarian women encompass the focus of this book since their culture is self-consciously African in its beliefs and practices. This Afrocentric perspective is necessary for any Diaspora movement; however, given the hierarchal nature of African societies, both past and present, a total acceptance of the African past is ill-advised.

As we look at different aspects of the feminist movement, we need to ask an important question—does one really exist? If we consider organizations that are working toward the betterment of women's economic and political status, groups that address domestic violence, and the rest, one might argue that there is a feminist movement. The problem is that the pieces of the movement are not working together to bring about a fundamental change in the political economy that gives rise to the various forms of abuses against women. In addition, many feminists have internalized the right (and the rite) of male privilege making it difficult to attack these problems head on.

What Lies Ahead?

This book is a result of many years of research in Jamaica—a place where I have come to feel somewhat at home. This feeling results in part from the strength I have gained from the lives that Rasta women have been willing to share with me and in part because a portion of my background is also Caribbean. In the course of my research, beginning in 1983, I have formally interviewed over one hundred women and have engaged in informal conversations with many more. These women, and some men, have welcomed me into their homes and into their lives in ways that I think is typical of many African people and in ways that have made my life richer. Having said that, it is important to note that not all Rastafarian women that I approached were willing to talk with me and a few thought that only Rasta should study Rasta. These few exceptions notwithstanding, I collected information from women in all of the fourteen regions of Jamaica.

Although Rasta women share some fundamental beliefs, there is a range of views and circumstances within this group. To the degree feasible, I share with you their own words regarding what it means to be a Rasta woman. These conversations are preceded by a broader discussion of the creation of Jamaican society beginning with the sixteenth century slave trade. A full understanding of the evolution of RastafarI is not possible outside of a consideration of the colonial, capitalist environment that spawned it.

Chapter 2 begins with a discussion of European suzerainty over the political and personal economies of Africans in Jamaica. Slave women were not only exploited for their labor but for the sexual services they were obliged to provide to European men. Mulatto offspring that resulted from these unions were given special privileges which increased the powerlessness of Africans in Jamaica. After emancipation, this privileged class formed alliances with planters and other capitalists. Racist ideologies promulgated by the English and their mulatto allies were internalized by many Africans who began to view themselves as inferior. Religious injunctions served as a fifth column in directing Jamaican's energies away from revolutionary endeavors.

In spite of this, a number of slaves used European religious ideology to organize rebellions to bring about their freedom. The emancipation of African slaves in 1838 did not fundamentally change their political or socio-economic condition which led to major rebellions by the working masses in the nineteenth and twentieth centuries.

Chapter 3 discusses the 1938 workers revolt, a watershed event which precipitated the formation of independence movements and political partisanship. During this same period Alexander Bustamante and Norman Manley rose to political stardom while attenuating demands from labor. Rastafarians, who had emerged several years prior to this, were concerned with nationalist and repatriation ventures and did not participate in larger struggles for *de facto* emancipation. The early days of RastafarI are significant in that they reveal the most radical period of the organization[5] which was later weakened as a result of government repression.

---

5. I use the word organization instead of movement here for two reasons: 1) many Rastas do not like to be referred to as a movement, and 2) given the lack of concrete gains made by Rastafarians, I do not think the term is appropriate.

Chapter 4 delineates the major Rastafarian houses (sects) and the position of women within these organizations. One of the important tenets omitted in most of the earlier works on Rasta is the belief in women's inferiority. Many Rasta men and women believe that the latter can only enter into Rastafarī through a man; men are considered the head of the household and the spiritual leaders of the organization. The belief that women's minds must be cultivated by men in order to understand the workings of Rastafarī underscores the degree of paternalism that exists. Attention is also given to other major tenets including repatriation, the belief in the divinity of Haile Selassie, and the divine nature of *ganja*.

Chapter 5 describes the general issue of sexism in Jamaica and identifies Rastafarī as one permutation of this institution. The focus here on political, economic, and cultural factors which systematically derogate women is key to understanding the systemic nature of sexism.

In addition to local control over women's mobility, multinational corporations proliferate under the aegis of the International Monetary Fund, increasing the GNP while simultaneously decreasing the standard of living for all poor Jamaicans, women being the hardest hit.

Chapter 6 outlines how the subordination of Rasta women is legitimized by religious rhetoric. It is written in the Bible that "man is the head of woman, just as god is the head of man." The spirit of this proclamation is pervasive in all of Jamaica, but is more strictly adhered to among Rastafarians. The concept of women's pollution derives, in part, from Biblical teachings and is employed by Rastas as the motivating force behind women's marginalization.

In Chapter 7, I discuss other symbols of identity which Rastas use as vehicles of protest. Their specialized language is combined with standard English in order to more closely reflect their identity as a neo-colonial people. Most prominent in what they call the Iyaric language is the substitution of "I" for prefixes of many words. The "I" replaces the objective form, me, and posits Rastas as active subjects.

Food habits also distinguish Rastas from other Jamaicans. As with other of their practices, foodways are derived from their belief in natural living and from their interpretations of the Christian Bible. Many Rastas are vegetarian and most attempt to maintain a diet as free from processed foods as possible. Even though they are ideologically dedicated to this way of life, necessity often wins over philosophy.

Hair and clothes play significant roles in defining Rastafarian identity and, more especially, in signifying the status of women. Some Rasta men can be distinguished by their dress, but almost all Rasta women are obliged to wear long skirts and head coverings. Proscriptions regarding women's dress provide an excellent vehicle for a discussion of the intersection between material and cultural containment.

Chapter 8 pays particular attention to the transformation of reggae from a music "of the people" to a music that is appealing and appeasing to commerical audiences. In addition, the production of reggae within a capitalist framework calls into question the role of reggae in "chanting down Babylon."

Ways in which Caribbean music, in general, and reggae in particular, have historically denigrated women is a central theme in this chapter. The negative representation of women in reggae and dance hall music is juxtaposed to the treatment of women in African American rap. While both reggae and rap have elements that are conscious and which underscore the institutionalization of racist imperialism, at the same time, they are inundated with misogynist themes.

Chapter 9 concludes this volume by addressing the development of RastafarI within a broader context of heterosexism and capitalist development in Jamaica. From my observations, Rastas are changing in many different directions. Even though there are some positive signs, on the whole, Rastas are becoming more diverse and less centralized. Rasta women, like women everywhere, are becoming more conscious, but this heightened consciousness characterizes the exceptions and not the masses.

Chapter 2

Slavery and Capitalism in Jamaica

Many people view Jamaica as a tourist paradise. Within this mythological context, Rastafarians are viewed as colorful, dreadlock wearing artifacts bearing "revolutionary" reggae music. In reality, Rasta emerged as a result of European colonialism in the western hemisphere and signifies a great deal more than dreadlocks and reggae. Rastas grew out of a complex process of slavery and slave resistence in Jamaica. In order to fully grasp the social and political-economic ramifications of RastafarI, an overview of slavery and neo-slavery in Jamaica is instructive.

There are a number of works that focus on the social history of slavery and capitalism in Jamaica (see, for example, Gray 1991; Williams 1961; Bush 1990). Without attempting to replicate this body of literature here, it is necessary to outline economic and political relations between Africans and Europeans at different stages in Jamaican history in order to understand the genesis of RastafarI.

Beginning in the sixteenth century, Jamaica became a major slave depot in the Caribbean. "From as early as 1517, Africans were brought to the island as household slaves to tend to the personal needs of their Spanish masters" (Beckford and Witter 1980:14). Indigenous Arawaks were also enslaved and subsequently wiped out by disease, terrorism and inhuman labor conditions (Black 1965:10–22 ff.; Patterson 1982:113). The English usurped the island from the Spanish in 1655 and soon established an active trade in slaves in order to develop a thriving plantation economy. As was the case on other Caribbean islands, African slaves fueled capitalist production and advanced the development of European economies. Between 1700 and 1786 more than 600,000 Africans were transported from the west coast of Africa primarily from the Igbo, Coromantee, Mandingo, Congo, Ashanti, and Akan peoples (Williams 1961:146).

In most of the Caribbean islands, including Jamaica, the number of female slaves slightly exceeded males (Higman 1984:308–310). The 1844 census recorded 293,128 Africans, 15,776 Europeans, and 68,549 colored people (Curtin 1955:240) on the island. This very stratified society was totally dependent on slave labor, financial and mechanical inputs from England, and on the palates of English consumers who craved the sugar produced by slaves.

At the beginning of the colonial era, sugar was the mainstay of the Jamaican economy. No part of the cane was wasted. Even bagasse, the

fibre portion of the sugar cane, was used as cattle feed and in the manufacture of particle board for house construction. Sugar was not only export-
ed to England as a sweetener but was also used in the manufacture of rum
and other alcoholic beverages.

By the end of the nineteenth century, rum was produced on over ninety eight percent of the 140 estates. Indeed, at this juncture, sugar was considered a by-product of rum since prices remained high for the latter and
continued to decline for the former.[1]

In 1675 there were approximately seventy sugar plantations in Jamaica.
From circa 1770 to 1775

> the slave population increased five-and-one-half-times; sugar output, eight-
> and-one-half times. In 1770 sugar and rum made up 87.7 percent of the
> value of all exports from Jamaica to Great Britain, Ireland, and North
> America which amounted to £1,538,730. Other exports in 1770 con-
> sisted of cotton, coffee, ginger, pimento, sarsaparilla, mahogany and hides
> (Sheridan 1989:63).

Surplus value from sugar production was appropriated by the English
in order to fuel their Industrial Revolution. The rebellion by the thirteen
colonies in reaction to taxation abuses led to the American Revolution and
signalled the decline of British imperialism in the western hemisphere. The
decline was due in part to the substantial loss of American food supplies
resulting in 15,000 slaves in Jamaica dying from famine between 1780
and 1787 (Post 1978:21). This, and competition in sugar production from
Haiti and Cuba, and beet sugar from Europe, also dealt a severe blow to
Jamaica's plantation economy.

In order to ensure high returns on sugar production, Africans in Jamaica
received poor rations and were made to live in conditions suited only for
animals. Slaves responded to these circumstances in a number of ways
including "sabotage, withdrawal of labour ("laziness"), protests in words
and in song, escape, and outright rebellion (Beckford and Witter 1980:18).
Nanny was one of the legendary women who led maroon communities in
their fight against British forces in the eighteenth century.

Although there were many instances of slave revolts in Jamaica one of
the most well known in the Antilles was Tacky's rebellion in 1760. Secrecy
and rituals that encompassed a syncretic blend of African practices were
integral to the formation of Tacky's forces. In particular Obeah, the practice of sorcery or magic that slaves brought with them from Africa, gave
inspiration to the rebellion (Brathwaite 1971:162).

---

1. After emancipation, freed slaves diversified their production of subsistence crops to
export commodities such as bananas, oranges, pineapples and tamarinds (Eisner
1961:170, 210–217).

Tacky, a Coromantee slave who had been an African chief, organized a group of men in Port Maria on Easter Monday and was successful in destroying a number of plantations and killing European settlers. Their surge was brought to a close when a slave from one of the overrun plantations reported the whereabouts of his team. The Maroons were primarily responsible for the capture of Tacky and his men. This was not surprising since they were obliged by the 1738 treaty with the English to aid in the capture of runaway slaves (Black 1965:93; Edwards 1973: 237–239; Campbell 1990:21). The English, realizing the central role that obeah had in fomenting rebellious activities across the country attempted to discourage other uprisings by persecuting obeah practitioners.

> On capturing an obeahmen who told the rebels that his power would pro-
> tect them in battle, the English hung him in a prominent place, painted
> and dressed up as he was in his mask, ornaments of teeth and bone and
> feather trimmings (Black 1973:93).

Even though this diminished the rebels' faith in the power of obeah, slave revolts continued throughout the island which resulted in the deaths of many Africans and Europeans. Punishment meted out to slaves for running away or for inciting revolts was savage. In addition to executions, many were severely beaten, burned alive, or starved to death. In spite of these reprisals, Africans continued to struggle for freedom.

Other slave revolts were occurring all over the Caribbean, the most successful being the Haitian Revolution in 1791. Other major uprisings included the 1816 revolt in Barbados (Beckles 1987:82) and the Berbice revolt in Guyana in 1763. Maroon societies in Surinam and Brazil are well known for their military prowess against the Dutch and the Portuguese, respectively. While rebellions took place throughout the slave era in Jamaica, the Christmas Rebellion of 1831 led by Sam Sharpe stands out among those that precipitated emancipation. The impetus for Sharpe's insurrection was Native Baptist teaching which promulgated equality and vilified the injustices of slavery (Genovese 1981:103). Sharpe, along with other Baptists and myal men[2] organized slaves in Treelawny, Westmoreland, St. James, St. Elizabeth, Hanover, and Manchester. Sharpe alleged that England had emancipated the slaves, but the Jamaican colonial government was unwilling to grant them their freedom. This expectation led the slaves to believe that British soldiers would not fire on them during the conflict. Alas, this

---

2. Obeah was a kind of witchcraft which Africans brought with them from the motherland. Obeah practitioners often induced slaves to insurrection which made the practice, "punishable by death. Myalism was a form of anti-witchcraft also derived from West Africa which slaves employed to counteract the evil effects of obeah" (Green 1976:30).

proved not to be the case. The English killed more than five hundred slaves (Curtin 1955:84–86) while European losses mostly consisted of damages to property[3]. Sharpe was hung on 23 May 1832. Even though he and his party were captured, his rebellion along with others, served as the impetus toward emancipation.

African Female Slaves in the Caribbean

It could be argued that women's oppression on the slave plantations was more pernicious than that of men since women not only suffered the degradation of slave labor and harsh punishment, but the humiliation of sexual abuse as well (Bush 1990; Brathwaite 1984).

The high rate of infertility and miscarriage among African slave women is indicative of the harsh conditions of slavery (Sheridan 1985:222–234). Many reasons have been offered for these occurrences including the hard labor that women had to endure, harsh punishments, and poor nutrition. That women who experienced these injustices also had high fertility rates, makes these propositions questionable. Other evidence suggests that it is more likely that women used herbal abortifacients (Bush 1990:140; Long 1970:346) or sharp sticks in order to save their children from the horrors of slavery. These self-induced abortions were one among many forms of resistance employed by women. Suicide, breaking tools (Campbell 1990:20), stealing property, and poisoning (Sheridan 1989) were also common forms of resistance. Punishments for these acts were often more harsh and more frequent than those meted out to men, even when women were pregnant. One planter noted that

> "[White overseers and bookkeepers...[kicked] [B]lack women in the belly from one end of Jamaica to another." (Williamson 1817:191 as quoted in Gaspar and Hine 1996:197)

In the heightened period of sugar cultivation from the 1670s until the 1740s, disregard for reproduction was common and mortality rates high. Pregnant women were kept in the field until a few weeks before delivery, then sent back no more than three weeks after, resulting in high rates of miscarriage, sterility, and poor health. Importing new slaves was more profitable than improving the conditions that would increase fertility.

Sexual abuse and rape were common as was the penchant to blame African women for these transgressions. Given the pervasive stereotypes

---

3. Total damage was estimated to be the destruction of 160 properties and twelve European casualties (Curtin 1955: 84–86).

that depicted African women as promiscuous and immoral, they were said to lure European men to their beds (Beckles 1995:125). This characterization allowed European men to rape African women with impunity while at the same time upholding the image of "white purity." Slave women were also used as breeders, their sole purpose being to produce more slaves (Steady 1987:9).

Since African women were their master's property, they were often exploited as prostitutes (Brathwaithe 1971:160). European men and women often acted as pimps and sold the sexual favors of slave women. Women's sexual subordination continued as many of them served as concubines to Europeans, successful mulattoes, or quadroons (Gaspar and Hine 1995:281). In some instances, concubinage conferred economic advantages on the women involved.

English men who committed adultery with colored women were not rebuked by European society, but marriage to these women was forbidden (Green 1976:20). The mulatto offspring from these unions were lighter than their mothers and were often given freedom, education, and other economic privileges. These progeny assumed the tastes and characteristics of the ruling class and often owned slaves themselves. Since many African slaves had also internalized the belief that people of European descent were their natural and cultural superiors, mulattoes, close in color and status to Europeans, were also paid deference.

Some of these mulattoes were able to acquire substantial amounts of real estate and other forms of capital. Many were businessmen, lawyers, preachers and teachers. In 1830 these free colored people were granted equality with people of European descent (Segal 1995:172) which allowed them to achieve financial mobility and to participate in electoral politics. This class served as a buffer between the European elites and Africans which meant that the relative economic success experienced by mulattoes was held up by Europeans as evidence of the former's superiority over Africans and as an example of largess on the part of Europeans. At the same time, Europeans remained in control of the island and could always threaten mulattoes with the same treatment meted out to Africans if the former stepped too far out of their place.

This racial stratification was the order of the day throughout the Caribbean islands. More significantly, the color/class dichotomy of the colonial period continued throughout the decades and remains in place in contemporary Jamaica. The vast majority of the mulatto class saw themselves as superior to the darker Africans and sought to maintain their color privilege by marrying endogamously or by "marrying White." In an effort to use their mixed heritage to their advantage, mulattoes, or "free Coloureds" often sided with European interests in order to gain social and economic mobility.

Christianity and Revivalist Religions

While many people claim that religion has been an opiate used to mollify the masses of African people, others suggest that it has been used by them as a catalyst in their fight for liberation. Contradictory as these two propositions may seem, both are true. Religious thought has encouraged many to look for their rewards in heaven or to believe that a god will solve their problems here on earth. At the same time, religion has served as the spiritual and ideological impetus to many resistance movements.

Most of the accounts of Christian missionary work in Jamaica were written by Europeans since most of the African and mulatto preachers of the time were illiterate. The Moravians were the first European missionaries to arrive in Jamaica in 1754. Originally from Czechoslovakia, Moravians were forced to emigrate to England where they established their missionary organizations.[4] In Jamaica they installed their missions primarily in St. Elizabeth, where many missionaries lived on estates and owned slaves. The Methodists followed in 1789 (Brathwaite 1971:252–253) led by Thomas Coke. The majority of the Methodist congregation encompassed "free coloureds" (Ibid 1971:208–209).

At the beginning of the nineteenth century, Church of England clergymen migrated to Jamaica in order to minister to European inhabitants. In the beginning, this church did not try to convert African slaves because they deemed them unworthy of conversion (Tarte-Booth 1984:16). Similar to claims of manifest destiny by Europeans in the United States, the Anglicans used their religious ideology to legitimate their hegemony on the island. Most Europeans were members of the Established Church of England (Anglican) whose mission in Jamaica was primarily to minister to European land owners. It was not until the decade before slavery ended that the Anglicans began to establish schools for Jamaicans of African descent and minister to slaves.

Baptist missionaries of African descent from the United States had a positive effect on African slaves in Jamaica. By the end of slavery, one half of the slave population had converted, in descending order, to Baptist, Methodist, and Moravian faiths. One of the first African American preachers from the United States was George Liele, a freed slave from Georgia who established the first Baptist church in Jamaica.

---

4. The Moravian Church came to Jamaica through two British plantation owners, William Foster and Joseph Foster-Barham. These two brothers had been converted by an evangelist in England and invited the church to establish a mission on their plantation. In 1754, the Moravian Church in England sent three missionaries, Zacharias George Caries, Thomas Shallcross, and Gottlieb Haberecht to Jamaica with the goal of preaching the gospel to slaves (Lewis, K. 1985).

Table 1	
Religious Affiliation in Kingston, 1825	
1 Established Church	(600 members, predominantly British)
2 Wesleyan Methodist	(3,400 members) 2/3 free African, 1/3 slave, a few Europeans (approx. 160)
2 Baptist	(2,000 members) 1/3 free, 2/3 slaves
1 Presbyterian	(1,250 members) 40–50 European, 100 Free African, the remainder, slaves
1 Catholic	(150) All Spanish and French speaking Europeans
(Gordon S. 1996:10)	

Liele transported the African foundations of religious life to Jamaica in naming his church the Ethiopian Baptist Church. African American Baptists focused on liberation themes and made frequent references to Africa. Naturally, the plantocracy was threatened by this Afrocentric focus and often arrested or deported the missionaries involved. The relative frequency with which African Jamaicans gravitated to the Baptist church in the early nineteenth century is indicated in Table 1.

In 1814 British Baptists arrived in Jamaica heavily influenced by the anti-slavery movement in Britain. The colonial government instructed these missionaries not to meddle in political-economic affairs. Nevertheless, most missionaries tried to educate African Jamaicans and emphasized the importance of self-worth. Many free coloreds and African Jamaicans became educated in a more general sense as a result of these mission activities.

After the British Act of Emancipation in 1833, European missionaries flourished. Their programs for education and conversion were now encouraged by the government (ostensibly to prepare slaves for freedom). Missionaries from the London Missionary Society arrived in 1834 and tried to spread the word to more remote districts; however, they encountered resistance from the Native Baptists, whom the missionaries often considered heathens (Ibid:14).

After Emancipation, British Baptist missionaries assumed more political roles and saw as their goal the production of a moral, respectable, free labor force. Even though Europeans appeared to be concerned over Africans' well-being, many of the very tenets they preached encouraged docility and obedience, and were thus a way to inveigh against rebellion. Generally speaking, European religious teachings did divert potential revolutionary energies, but in many cases, Christian ideology also served as a catalyst for protest. In addition, Jamaicans used these missions to gain an education, after which some of them formed their own churches. A number of African Jamaicans continued to practice Myalism (spirit worship) and other African derived religions which constituted another major impetus to revolt.

The fact that RastafarI protest is couched in religious terms is not new to Jamaica since the eighteenth and nineteenth century expressions of resistance were spurred by religious teachings. Myalism was the predominant form of African religion in Jamaica when the missionaries began to arrive. It was a conglomeration of several different African belief systems brought to the slave estates, and included the belief in a supreme god. However, more influential than god were the ancestral spirits and forces of nature. Jamaican slaves believed that these spirits could possess one in dreams and ritual dances. Funeral rites constituted a particularly important aspect of myal practices since participants believed that the spirit of the departed would remain among them (as a duppie, or evil spirit) for nine days after death. Thus, ceremonies were performed to return the dead to their ancestral home in Africa. Another important function of myalism was to counteract *obeah*, another African derivative that was practiced mostly by African-born women and men.

Obeah involved conjuring up spirits to harm, or even kill, others. Europeans feared that Obeah men would poison them. Moreover, Obeah leaders were known to foment rebellion among the slaves and thus posed a formidable threat to planters. One of the earliest slave revolts that was heavily influenced by obeah, as was mentioned earlier, was Tacky's revolt in 1760.

Secrecy and rituals were used to galvanize anti-slavery emotions and African solidarity (Brathwaite 1971:162). Obeah was outlawed in 1781 and could carry the death penalty if plots against Europeans were suspected (Gordon S. 1996:47). Myalism and Kumina were also banned by the colonial government as was traditional African drumming and dancing. Nevertheless, African cultural forms persisted by incorporating beliefs and practices into Christian rituals. Even given this syncretism, many myalists saw themselves as superior to

> more orthodox Christians and to civil authorities, even to the extent of denouncing the queen, remarkable at a time when no matter what was thought of all other whites, the queen was venerated as a figure of superhuman benevolence (Stewart 1992:144).

Myalism and Baptist teachings had several beliefs in common, for example, baptism by immersion and receiving the holy spirit were common to both religions. This blending of African and Christian beliefs culminated in the formation of Zion and Pukkumina[5] churches, which still have a powerful influence among working class people of Jamaica.

---

5. Pukkumina has been customarily spelled as Pocomania, which translates from Spanish to "little madness". However, there is no proof of any Spanish linkage or derivation of the religion. Most likely, Pukkumina is more closely linked semantically with Kumina (Seaga 1969:4).

	1943	1960
Population	1,240,000	1,610,000
Pukkumina	.07	.01
Zion	.41	No Data

Table 2
Percentage of Revivalists in Jamaica

Source: Census figures reformulated from Seaga (1982:5).

Barrett (1988:16) notes that Pukkumina was adapted from Kumina, an African religion, where elaborate drumming, rituals, and spirit possession are major customs. According to 1943 and 1960 census figures only a small percentage of Jamaicans participated in Revivalist practices (see Table 2). According to Seaga (1982:5) these figures are grossly underestimated. Revivalism is viewed disparagingly by a wide sector of the Jamaican population, a perspective which forces many revivalists to conceal their affiliation with these groups.

Seaga reports that there were more women members in Revivalist groups than men. Women could hold leadership positions in either religion, but Zionists tended to have more male leaders (1982:5). Male leaders were called Captain and female leaders, Mother. According to public opinion, male leaders were said to have many female sexual partners within the group (Ibid: 12).

Pukkumina and Zion religions are pertinent to our discussion of Rasta since Rastafarl and revivalists have maintained African dimensions to their ritual practices. Moreover, many of the early Rastafarians were formerly members of Zion or Pukkumina churches. Even though many Rastafarians used drumming in their ceremonies, they are unlike revivalists in that they were concerned with racial and economic factors in addition to their religious focus. For a more in depth look at religious historical development in Jamaica, see Morrish (1982) and Turner (1982).

Post-Emancipation Slaves

The vast majority of Africans in the Caribbean remained tied to former slave masters; however, alternatives to plantation labor varied from island to island. During slavery some Jamaican slaves earned income from harvests from provision grounds provided by the planters. Others bought property in the interior and worked land for their own subsistence (Vergne 1994:15). After slavery many former slaves were able to purchase land on income earned during slavery from harvests on their own provision grounds. Even though many poor people owned and cultivated small holdings, these were not adequate enough to allow them a decent standard of living. Thus, small landowners were compelled to work for meager wages. Others acquired land that was abandoned by former slave masters or merely squatted on unoccupied territory. Many planters charged rents to landless Jamaicans, thereby compelling former slaves to remain in a virtual state of bondage. If more than one person lived in a household, each household member was charged a hut tax, thus maximizing control over freed slaves. Some former slaves migrated to urban areas in order to supplement plantation work.

Women, who constituted the majority of field workers at the time of emancipation, were eager to leave the plantations to spend more time with their families and to earn money elsewhere. Planters, however, were shrewd in their efforts to contain these laborers. In spite of efforts to contain women's labor, they dominated the marketing system that

> developed during slavery and supported themselves and their families by higgling[6] in produce markets or selling wares on the street, thus abandoning plantation labor altogether or performing certain tasks when wages rose during the harvest. Less frequently, women became permanently established as school teachers, small landowners, or business managers (Vergne 1994:15).

Even though former slaves struggled to find ways to eke out a living, the abolition of slavery did not change their access to the means of production. Thus, working class and middle class Jamaicans continued to be subordinated to European colonial rule. Despite middle class efforts to protest racial and economic exploitation, their plans were compromised by a paradoxical blend of anti-colonial sentiment and the adoption of European colonial values. The development of a middle class nationalist consciousness was also attenuated by their inability to take up the cause of the working class.

> Where the [small entrepreneurs and the professionals] found an unstable and contested niche in commerce and the bureaucracy, the laboring classes bore the brunt of the economic hardship produced by the underdeveloped nature of Jamaica's capitalism (Gray 1991:19).

---

6. Higgling refers to small scale, self-employment.

Africans remained dependent on their former masters who owned the best and largest tracts of land. Large scale growers and multinational corporations such as the sugar empire of Tate and Lyle, and banana companies owned by United Fruit Company maintained control over the means of production thereby perpetuating the relations of production that prevailed during slavery. Their usurpation of small peasant holdings created an impoverished rural proletariat and pushed others into urban centers. The elite maintained their advantage by doling out meager wages and importing East Indian workers to counter any demands from former slaves.

Along with low wages and chronic unemployment, former slaves were subject to poor medical and sanitary conditions. The latter was so severe that the cholera epidemic in 1850–1851 killed between twenty-five and thirty thousand laborers. Thousands more succumbed to the smallpox epidemic which came on the heels of the cholera outbreak. In addition to these scathing episodes, chronic malnutrition and hookworm were common (Curtin 1955:160). Thus, even with emancipation, former slaves were totally captured within a colonial plantocracy that paid no heed to their economic or physical needs.

In addition, African Jamaicans had no legal redress to the inequities of this system since local and national governments did everything possible to thwart social and economic change. It was against these conditions that Paul Bogle, a Baptist preacher, and his party protested in 1865. Bogle's revolt, which resulted in the deaths of many Europeans and many more Africans, highlighted the racial foundations of their oppression which was indicated in his jeremiads, "Blood, blood, we must humble the white man before us," (as quoted in Campbell 1990:38) and "Cleave to the Black."

Bogle's army is much written about, but very few scholars have chosen to include the women who played active roles in this rebellion. They attacked men in Morant Bay Square, and raided police stations for guns and ammunition. The most notable female figures in this rebellion were Rosanna Finlayson, Caroline Grant, and Sarah Johnson. Johnson was clearly in step with Bogle's cry to "Cleave to the Black" since on her way to Morant Bay, she proclaimed that "every mulatto was to be killed as well as the white man" (Government Papers, Commission by Governor Eyre:354–355, as quoted in Wilmot 1995:291).

Bogle and his army were eventually captured, but what is significant about his resistance ideology is that it was one of the few revolts in the nineteenth century (or since) that actually sought to overthrow European rule by any means necessary. Former maroons, who earlier posed a potential threat to the slavocracy, were one of the pivotal forces in the final defeat of Bogle's troops. Bogle's race-based revolt also heightened the mulattoes' allegiance to the English regime. In 1862 one of their newspapers reported,

> Let the colored men of Jamaica be true to themselves and their progress
> will be certain; their best policy is to form a bond of union with the white
> brethren, and if this is done, no Governor will presume to keep from them
> the rights to which they are entitled as loyal subjects of the sovereign of
> Great Britain (Curtin 1955:175).

After emancipation, landed and landless laborers continued to fuel the
economies of Jamaican and foreign elite. At the close of the nineteenth
century, low wages and high unemployment led many workers to migrate
to Panama, Costa Rica, and Cuba. Working conditions in these countries
were also deplorable and subjected laborers to high rates of disease and slave
wages (Petras 1988). The fact that Jamaicans continued to subject themselves to this abuse was a reflection of the lack of viable options in Jamaica.

> For those who emigrated, the promises of a wage as well as food and
> housing on a contractual basis seemed preferable to the semislavery or
> unemployment into which they had been forced during and after Appren-
> ticeship (Petras 1988:68).

Marcus Garvey

Laborers who remained in Jamaica protested against miserable working conditions and low pay. They employed a variety of strategies including strikes and grievances against retail merchants. In particular, African
Jamaicans saw Chinese laborers, along with Syrians and other foreigners,
as a barrier to employment and business opportunities (see Post:210–211
and Gray 1991:15–16 passim). Marcus Garvey, who later laid the ideological framework for the formation of RastafarI, was one of the leading
advocates for better wages and working conditions for workers.

Garvey was born in St. Ann's Bay, Jamaica in 1887. During his early
years, he worked as a printer in Kingston and, by the time he was twenty,
became a master printer and foreman at one of the largest Jamaican firms,
the P.A. Benjamin Company (Cronon 1955:12). When the Printer's Union
struck for higher wages, Garvey was quickly elected to lead the strike. The
strike ended, however when the employers began to introduce linotype
machines and imported printers to operate them. Most of the striking
printers were able to return to their jobs, but Garvey, as the only foreman
who had joined the strike, found himself blacklisted and was forced to
leave the island.

Garvey subsequently travelled to Nicaragua, Ecuador, Honduras,
Columbia, and Venezuela and witnessed the oppression of African people in these countries. In 1909 he travelled to Costa Rica and started a
newspaper, *La Nacion*, in order to protest these atrocities. He made similar efforts in Panama through *La Prensa* but was unsuccessful due to the

lack of organization among workers. From Central America Garvey returned to Jamaica for a brief period and subsequently travelled to England where his political education was broadened. In 1912 he travelled to London where he met Duse Mohammed Ali in London and worked on Ali's *African Times and Orient Review*. Ali encouraged Garvey to read widely in history and culture, especially regarding African peoples. One of the most influential works that Garvey read during this period was the life and works of Booker T. Washington. So impressed was he with Washington's Tuskegee machine, that Garvey decided to create an organization fashioned after Washington's Tuskegee Institute.

In addition to the Tuskegee model, Garvey's disenchantment with struggles to improve labor conditions in Jamaica and his emergent pan-Africanist philosophy led him in 1914 to form the United Negro Improvement and Conservation League. This organization, which later came to be known as the United Negro Improvement Association (UNIA), sought to encourage African Jamaicans to develop their own institutions and struggle for self-determination. So forceful was Garvey's challenge that neo-colonial leaders undermined his efforts to organize in Jamaica. These developments led Garvey to resuscitate the UNIA in New York City in 1917 where he began the largest movement of Diaspora Africans in history.

Garvey promulgated three primary tenets: 1) racial pride, 2) self-sufficiency of African descended people, and 3) repatriation of diaspora Africans to Africa. These goals were fundamental to a people who had been materially and culturally marginalized and laid the ground work for liberation struggles in Africa and the African Diaspora (Lewis 1988; Lewis 1994; Martin 1976; 1983). Even though Garvey attracted a large following in the United States, the Caribbean, and Africa, a number of more moderate diaspora Africans, most notably, William E.B. DuBois, A. Philip Randolph, and Cyril Briggs undermined his efforts (Garvey 1978:71–72 passim; Cronon 1955:99–101;106–107;196).

In spite of this opposition Garvey was successful in establishing the *Black Star Line* in 1919 and purchased two ships that he named the *SS Frederick Douglass* and the *SS Antonio Maceo*. In 1924 he incorporated another company, the *Black Cross Navigation and Trading Company*, and acquired the *SS Goethals* which he subsequently renamed the *SS Booker T. Washington*. Through the *Black Star Line*, Garvey transported commodities and passengers from the Caribbean and the United States to Africa, but he did not succeed in transporting the masses of diaspora Africans to Africa that he had planned. The reasons were two-fold. Garvey's ships went aground as a result of the poor condition of the vessels and poor management of funds on the part of *Black Star Line* employees. The demise of the steamship companies was also accelerated by the efforts of William E.B. DuBois.

DuBois, who has been given the label "the Father of Pan-Africanism," was staunchly opposed to Garvey's idea of repatriating diaspora Africans to Africa. By 1921 Garvey had made substantial progress toward repatriation and succeeded in sending delegations to Liberia to secure land for settlement. In 1924 DuBois, travelled to Liberia and convinced President King to discontinue negotiations with Garvey and the UNIA. As a result, members of the UNIA were deported and their shipment of supplies was confiscated. Not only was DuBois opposed to Garvey's back-to-Africa emphasis, but he declared that "African Americans would not be able to stand the heat in Africa" (*New York Tribune,* Sept 6, 1921 as reported in Garvey 1978:71).

During this same period, the United States government, which was also threatened by Garvey's program, was pressuring Garvey on many fronts. At the culmination of a relentless pursuit, Garvey was convicted of mail fraud[7] on February 2, 1925 and began serving his sentence in the United States penitentiary in Atlanta, Georgia. In 1927 President Calvin Coolidge commuted his sentence and deported him to Jamaica. In 1929, Garvey formed the People's Political Party, the first political party in Jamaica.

While he used this platform to advocate for a more representative government, he also tried to resuscitate his repatriation movement but was imprisoned for contempt charges. In 1935 he migrated to London and once again attempted to revive his program but was not successful in this regard. On June 10, 1940 Garvey died of a stroke. Ironically William E.B. DuBois, who had spent concerted energy in deriding Garvey's back to Africa movement, felt compelled to emigrate to Ghana in 1963 where he lived out the last years of his life.

Although Garvey did not realize all of his goals, he rekindled Diaspora African pride in African identity. He emphasized that all people worshiped their own god and that African descended people should also worship a god in their own image—a Black god. These notions were crucial in creating a counterhegemonic ideology among diaspora Africans since a people are bound to see themselves as inferior if their god is represented in someone else's image. Garvey suggested that

> [w]e Negroes believe in the God of Ethiopia, the ever-lasting God, god the father, God the son, and the Holy ghost, the One god of all ages. That is the God in whom we believe, but we shall worship Him through the spectacles of Ethiopia (Garvey 1967:34).

---

7. Garvey was charged and convicted for mail fraud, although the key piece of evidence was a Black Star Line envelope that supposedly contained promotional circulars to prospective subscribers. The envelope presented was empty, and the recipient, Benny Dancy, could not recall clearly what the envelope had contained (Cronon 1955: 115).

These concepts were not new to Jamaicans or other diaspora Africans since the Bible made frequent reference to Ethiopia and Egypt. Thus Garvey's emphasis on diaspora African repatriation and a Black god infused the ranks of many Jamaicans who were already mired in Christian ideology and the concept of Ethiopia as the ancestral land. This notion of a Black god is central to the development of self-esteem among a people who had been taught for centuries that they were inferior. Whether a Black god (or any god) is real or imaginary is less important than the fact that this image counteracted the colonizers' image of a White god that validated the African's servile position. Afrocentric religious ideology is important because it

> counterbalance[s] the profound sense of loss...To describe as myths these forms of remembering, of constructing new shared identities, and of formulating particular visions of the future is not necessarily to dismiss them as illegitimate aspirations, false versions of history, or invalid types of identity, but rather to emphasize their *social* (emphasis in original) character....Myths are not relics of some antique past, but mechanisms for organizing experience and reworking the present (Sorenson 1992:201).

It is important to note here that Garvey's philosophy not only influenced Rastafarians, but other diaspora Africans as well, including such groups as the Nation of Islam, established in 1930, and Father Divine's Peace Mission in which George Baker (1880–1965) declared himself to be a god. Not parenthetically, some of the early Rasta leaders, e.g. Claudius Henry, Leonard Howell, and later Prince Emmanuel, came to think of themselves as "god" or the returned Christ.

Garvey was not a Rastafarian, but laid the ideological framework for the formation of this group. His emblematic colors, red, black and green, are the Rastafarian symbols which signify, respectively: the blood shed by African people in their struggle for freedom; African people in all parts of the globe; and the homeland of Africa. Rastas have added the color yellow which signifies Jamaica. They also internalized the notion of back-to-Africa as a redemptive strategy for diaspora Africans.

The Crowning of Lij Tafari Makonnen

The marginalized position of working class Jamaicans created fertile ground for the cultivation of Garvey's message. When Garvey left Jamaica for the United States in 1916, there remained a number of individuals who formed Garveyite movements. Many of Garvey's followers who began to look to Africa for their salvation also looked to the Bible for guidance. The Bible predicted that "Princes shall come out of Egypt, and Ethiopia shall stretch

forth her hands unto God" (Psalms 68:30). The crowning of Lij Tafari
Makonnen (also known as Ras Tafari) as the Emperor Haile Selassie of
Ethiopia in 1930 led many Jamaicans to interpret this event as a fulfilled
prophecy. The fact that Haile Selassie claimed to be a direct descendant of
David and referred to himself as King of Kings, Lord of Lords and Conquering
Lion of Judah gave a small sector of Jamaicans further credence in his divinity. Selassie was aware of his veneration by Rastafarians, but never proclaimed himself to be a god or the leader of the group. Even though the vast
majority of people of African descent did not consider Haile Selassie to be
a god, large numbers of Diaspora and continental Africans were ready to lay
down their lives to protect him and his country upon Mussolini's 1935 invasion (Asante 1977).

African Americans organized the Committee for the Defense of Ethiopia.
They also added to the ideological ferment in Jamaica by sending literature
on African and diaspora African history. Organizations in Africa and the
African diaspora employed a number of strategies in their attempts to oust
Mussolini including mass prayers, boycotting Italian-made products, and
forming military cadres to fight in Ethiopia. Men of African descent in
many parts of the African Diaspora were prepared to go to battle for
Ethiopia. Although Jamaicans proposed to send a battalion of men to
Ethiopia (Post 1978:168), nothing came of this due to resistance by Jamaica's
colonial government. Mussolini's invasion also brought together conti-
nental and diaspora Africans who were living in Europe. Many of the
African organizations who were willing to take up arms were organized in
London, Nigeria, and Ghana. Not surprisingly, the British colonial gov-
ernment counteracted these moves by reviving the almost forgotten Foreign
Enlistment Law of 1870 which

> forbade British subjects and 'natives' of a British Protectorate to join forces
> of countries—in this case, Italy and Ethiopia—which maintained friend-
> ly relations with Britain (Asante 1977:140).

While continental and diaspora Africans were using every means at their
disposal to aid in bringing about Ethiopia's independence, Haile Selassie
fled his country and took refuge in England on 3 June 1936. When Italy
was finally expunged from Ethiopia as a result of her defeat in World War
II, Selassie returned home in 1941.

In an effort to recognize diaspora African commitment to Ethiopia during the Italian invasion, Haile Selassie sent his cousin, Malaku Bayen, to
New York to establish The Ethiopian World Federation (EWF). Bayen
founded the organization on August 25, 1937 for the purpose of enhanc-
ing unity among African people.

> We, the Black People of the World, in order to effect Unity, Solidarity,
> Liberty, Freedom and self-determination, to secure Justice and maintain

the Integrity of Ethiopia, which is our divine heritage, do hereby establish and ordain this constitution for the Ethiopian World Federation, Inc. (The Constitution and By-Laws of the Ethiopian World Federation, 1937, p. 4. as quoted in Smith et al. 1960:9).

The following EWF principles are indicative of its pan-African focus.

1. The unity of Blacks in all parts of the world;
2. Financial and moral support of Ethiopia and Ethiopian refugees;
3. Definite action as a united whole against wrongs perpetrated against members of the race in any part of world;
4. Demand for the continental independence and full sovereignty of Ethiopia;
5. Ethiopia for Ethiopians at home and abroad;
6. No surrender to Italian aggression in Ethiopia;
7. To aid Ethiopians in their determined and never failing campaign to expel Italians from Ethiopia; and
8. To prepare our people to take their rightful place among the nations of the earth (Voice of Ethiopia, May 1938 as quoted in Campbell 1990:76).

The first Jamaican branch was established in 1938 under the leadership of Paul Earlington and one Mr. Mantle, as Vice-President and President, respectively. Even though there were Rastafarians who had a loose affiliation with the EWF, it was not a Rastafarian organization. Like Rastas, the EWF was androcentric with few women in leadership positions. A one Ms. Green,[8] was appointed as President of one of the Jamaican branches only as a compromise appointment between two male rivals (see Smith et al. 1960:10). Apparently Maymie Richardson figured prominently in the organization in the 1950s, but scholars who were familiar with the organization did not consider it important enough to elaborate on her activities. According to Smith (1960:12), there was also an all-women's branch (Local 41), but no other information regarding the members or their activities are given.

The EWF in Jamaica was loosely affiliated with other race conscious organizations like the African Nationalist Movement, the Ethiopian Youth Cosmic Faith, the United Afro-West Indian Brotherhood, and several other groups that emerged in the 1940s and 1950s (Campbell 1990:10).

The organization's newspaper, *The Voice of Ethiopia*, delivered a pan-African message which asserted that "Ethiopia Must be Free, Blackman Must be Free." Notwithstanding the androcentric focus in this slogan, this literary organ emphasized the commonality of African and Diaspora African struggles for liberation. The *Voice of Ethiopia* also proclaimed that the true

---

8. Unfortunately, the report does not consistently use a member's first and last names. Hence the names are used here just as they are cited in the literature.

Israelites were African and that Africans were the Twelve Tribes of Israel. Rastafarians, who were already at the helm in declaring themselves African people, readily accepted this banner. In spite of the cross fertilization between some Rasta and EWF organizations, the latter began to proclaim its distance from the Rastas when Claudius Henry became known for his plans for a violent overthrow of the Jamaican government (Smith 1960:31).

Even though the Ethiopian World Federation was established in order to create a bridge between African and the African Diaspora, it failed to sustain membership due to a lack of viable programs and an elitist leadership which doled out directives to the locals. At the same time, Rastafarianism, beginning with a small group of people in the early 1930s, continued to appeal to the disenfranchised and to grow in number for the next few decades.

In the early 1930s Leonard Howell, Joseph Hibbert, Archibald Dunkley, Robert Hinds, and Claudius Henry were leading exponents who promoted Haile Selassie as the divine Redeemer of African people. All four leaders established communities prophesying the divinity of Haile Selassie. Archibald Dunkley established the King of Kings Missionary Movement, Hibbert spread the word at his Ethiopian Coptic Church, and Howell promulgated the message through the Ethiopian World Federation. Claudius Henry established the African Reform Church in Kingston.

The background of these original Rastafarians and the details of their organizations have been well recorded (see, for example, Chevannes 1995; Barrett 1988). Therefore, my intention here is not to repeat the social history of these leaders, but to present an overview of some of the major events. While early Rasta leaders differed in their organizational style and political leanings, they had in common the desire to be free from colonial rule and the quest for self-determination.

Howell reportedly fought in the Ashanti War of 1896 in Ghana, West Africa as part of the British West India regiment (Barrett 1977:82). Hibbert travelled to Central America and became a member of the Ancient Order of Ethiopia, a Masonic Lodge, while in Costa Rica. Dunkley worked as a seaman with the Atlantic Fruit Company (Smith, Augier and Nettleford 1967:6). Henry spent several years in the United States where he was exposed to EWF and African American civil rights ideology. Clearly all of these men, like Garvey, were able to see the common features of racial, economic, and political oppression in other parts of the Diaspora. That all of them also espoused a theory of self-determination was a logical extension of their pan-African experience.

Leonard Howell was the seminal figure who laid the ideological framework for the organization. According to the literature, Howell began to proselytize the movement in 1933 by making copies of a photo of Haile Selassie which he sold for a shilling a piece as a passport to Ethiopia. Howell also laid out the principles of the movement:

(1) hatred for the White race; (2) the complete superiority of the Black race; (3) revenge on Whites for their wickedness; (4) the negation, persecution, and humiliation of the government and legal bodies of Jamaica; (5) preparation to go back to Africa; and (6) acknowledging Emperor Haile Selassie as the Supreme Being and only ruler of Black people (Barrett 1977:85).

The colonial government was not about to tolerate Howell's anti-government rhetoric sentenced him to two years in prison for inciting hatred and sedition among the Jamaican masses.[9] On 3 January 1934 Robert Hines, Howell's deputy, was sentenced to one year. In attempts to completely squelch the rise of Rastafarl, Archibald Dunkley and Joseph Hibbert were also arrested. Upon release, Howell and his followers gained more members and orchestrated their move from the hills of St. Catherine to a commune called *The Pinnacle*. It was at the Pinnacle that Rastas began to identify themselves as Nyabingi, a name borrowed from an anti-colonial group in Uganda, East Africa (Campbell 1980:7). It was also during this period that members of Howell's group began wearing dreadlocks. There is some debate as to where the idea of dreadlocks originated (see Chapter 7), but most sources indicate that they were adopted from the group's knowledge of dreadlocks worn by Masai warriors. Reportedly, the consumption of *ganja* among Rastafarians also began at the Pinnacle.

Even though Rastafarian symbols represented self-determination for Africans in Jamaica, Rastafarians did not, on the whole, actually participate in political or labor movements organized by other Jamaicans. In the 1930s several Rastafarian leaders established themselves and promulgated a philosophy in terms of race and religion that was at odds with that of the general populace. Throughout the ensuing decades Rastas were to evolve from a radical separatist stance to one where they peacefully advocated for repatriation. Although a few Rastas even attempted to participate in local politics, as a group, they were disengaged from the political struggles of the masses of working class people.

---

9. Howell was imprisoned for the second time in April 1937. For further details of his encounters with police and judicial system see Post (1978).

Chapter 3

The Political Economy of Jamaica, 1938–1997

The 1938 Rebellion

During the post-emancipation period, the planters' obsession with profit created conditions no better than during slavery. Minimum wage laws and regulations for the number of hours worked were nonexistent. According to a colonizer's records "it would take a worker 6 days to be able to afford a loaf of bread" (as quoted in Campbell 1990:80).

> Report followed report in tragi-comic succession, commenting on appalling conditions of the people, the undernourishment and malnutrition of children and the absence of rudimentary social services. Hookworm, yaws, beri-beri, scurvy and rickets accounted for a considerable measure of disability, and the absence of clean running water led to numerous bowel diseases (Ibid:80).

The revolt against these atrocities began with agricultural workers on sugar estates located throughout the island and quickly spread as factory, sanitation, and dock workers joined the strike. Inadequate housing, low pay, unexplained wage deductions, and unemployment added more fuel to the uprising. Alexander Bustamante and Norman Manley, two rising political stars who were to become major political figures in the ensuing decades, attempted to settle the problems of urban workers and peasant farmers; however, the forces of oppression had been too long in the making to easily placate their protests (Eaton 1975).

The workers began their demonstrations with strikes and rallies in Westmoreland[1] and later spread to other parishes. In Kingston demonstrators looted Chinese stores and "respectable" looking people, blocked roads, and overturned trash bins into the streets (Post 1978:280). Colonial forces ordered police and British forces stationed in Jamaica to put down the protest with rifles and machine guns. The demonstrators responded by stoning the police, but, of course, were held in check by superior military technology. Police killed several women, men, and children. Despite this repression, workers continued their offensive.

---

1. See Post (1978) for a detailed account of the 1938 Rebellion.

Rastafarians, as was true for many members of the working class, did not participate in the 1938 Rebellion (Williams 1986:12). The general thrust of RastafarI was to focus on repatriation to Africa and everlasting life here on earth. The pivotal figure in bringing about this state of perfection was believed to be the Emperor Haile Selassie, who was seen as a living god with supernatural characteristics. Even though Rastas expressed an anti-colonial and anti-White rhetoric, they also

> indulged in the highest degree of fantasy. There was thus an antagonistic contradiction within the cult at the cognitive level between the retreat implicit in refocusing upon redemption by Ras Tafari and the initial response of its members to the material reality of the social relations of exploitation (Post 1978:192–193).

Rastas emphasized the uneven race relations in 1936 and 1937 with their slogan "skin for skin and colour for colour" but did not mobilize with others of the working class who actively participated in the rebellion. Other factions of the working class were on the move.

In Spanish Town, sanitary workers led the charge which escalated into a more general strike.

> ...on Caymanas sugar estate, strikers blocked the entrance to the estate on the 25th [of May] and were fired on by Special Constables, four being wounded. In reprisal the cane was set on fire. Other sugar and banana estates in St. Catherine were struck, and public works labourers downed tools throughout the parish. In Montego Bay the dockers went on strike on hearing the news from Kingston, and A.G.S. Coombs led a hunger march of the unemployed to see the Superintendent of Public Works (Post 1978:281).

Workers in other parishes picked up the gauntlet, burning plantations, blocking roads, cutting telephone wires — using every tactic possible to disrupt Jamaican infrastructure and to call attention to their plight. Eventually Bustamante and Manley were effective arbitrators of the conflict between labor and capital and succeeded in quelling the revolt. Sugar companies increased wages and banana workers received small plots of land, but the basic condition of the urban workers and the rural proletariat had not changed. Bustamante and Manley had succeeded in gaining the faith of the masses, but had done so by convincing them to put down their arms — machetes, sticks, and stones. This admonition to work within the existing colonial order combined with the government's superior military technology effectively contained the revolt.

Even though small gains were made, the strikers did not confront the fundamental problem of lack of control over land and subjugation by foreign colonial forces. Indeed, the workers allegiance to the English crown was unquestionable as evidenced by their singing "God Save the King" at their labor rallies.

While working class resistance posed a potential threat to the colonial elite, workers on the whole did not develop mass movements or a viable plan that would extricate them from their predicament. In addition to the military power of the colonial regime, a combination of racist and Christian ideologies served as a counterforce to rebellious tendencies. Racist ideology which blamed Africans for their own enslavement by deeming them inferior was internalized by the masses as was Christian dogma which convinced them to wait on Judgement Day for their liberation. While they protested against the power of the elite and middle class, at the same time, they aspired to acquire material and cultural symbols of prestige. Deference paid to the upper classes was inconsistent with mounting an effective revolution. The absence of an effective plan that would change their relationship to the means of production was most obvious in the 1938 worker's revolt. The conservative undertones of this revolt were also reflected in policies targeted toward women. Men felt threatened by women's participation in the revolt at any level and by their visibility in its aftermath (Reddock 1984; French and Ford-Smith 1986).

Women and the 1938 Rebellion

Even though women fully participated in the 1938 Rebellion, their reward was a decrease in women's rights, a sharp decline in employment, and a general subjugation to the "male breadwinner concept" (French 1988:38–61). The male breadwinner concept was played against the female homemaker ideal—a dichotomy which was not new to Jamaica, but one which intensified after 1938.

Soon after the rebellion the colonial government commissioned Lord Moyne to conduct a survey of the British Caribbean and recommend reform strategies. In an attempt to establish a formal policy regarding the status of women, the Moyne Report[2] created a number of prescriptions that had a direct impact on women's social status and political-economic mobility.

During the period of reform, women sought to become more politically involved. Middle class women attempted to get elected to political offices, and poor working women actively participated in union activities. Their efforts, however, were met with resistance by the colonial government and also by men within their own ranks (Reddock 1984; French and

---

2. Following the 1938 Rebellion the colonial government ordered that a study be conducted which would outline the conditions of the working class and reform measures to ameliorate their condition. The result was a series of recommendations put forth by the West India Royal Commission which was chaired by Lord Moyne. The commission is commonly referred to as the Moyne Commission.

Ford-Smith 1986). While a few women were elected to the Legislative Council, they were not given financial support that would have enabled them to properly serve their constituencies. In addition to male resistance, there was evidence of class struggle among the women themselves. The degree to which middle-class women had internalized the pervasive negative perception of African descended women is witnessed by the fact that they fought against giving the vote to illiterate people and did not support Universal Adult Suffrage! In addition to their political marginalization, women's economic position also declined.

At the time of Emancipation, women were primarily employed in the field of agriculture. After the 1938 Rebellion, women's employment in agriculture precipitously declined while employment rates for men in the same field increased absolutely and relatively (French and Ford-Smith 1986:39). Women's employment also declined in other areas as a result of a Moyne Commission policy which sought to relegate women's work to the household. The Commission proposed that a woman's place was in the home and her dependency on a husband would ameliorate the problems of poverty. "If women were poor and families destitute, it was argued, it was because they did not have families with a man at the centre.... Where there was no father..." (French 1988:40),

> the whole (financial) responsibility falls on the mother... In such circumstances cases of extreme poverty are inevitable, for the standard of living must be lower than it would be in a family group where, even if both parents were not employed, more money would be available, since the wages of men are normally higher than those given to women (Moyne Commission Report 1938:221).

Thus women were expected to stay at home and reproduce the capitalist labor force and become dependent on their male partners. Even though I am not suggesting that viable solutions exist within a capitalist framework, clearly the idea of paying women adequate wages so that they could support themselves apparently never occurred to the Commission.

The primary vehicle for the realization of the Moyne Report was the Colonial Development and Welfare Office (CDWO). The Jamaican Women's Federation (JWF), formed in 1944, came under the auspices of the CDWO and was modeled after the Women's Institute of Great Britain. The JWF was an important vehicle for the perpetuation of Jamaican patriarchy since it promoted the concept of women as homemakers and the centrality of the nuclear family with men as the sole breadwinners.

The reactionary nature of this organization is reflected in its main activities which included Homemaker's Day, a kitchen-garden competition, and the Better Home campaign. The latter was devised in order to promote the ideal of two-parent families. In order to augment this institution, the JWF organized mass weddings. Rings could be purchased for ten shillings so that hundreds of women and men could be married in a single ceremony. The emphasis on marriage and nuclear families is not as problematic as the fact that these institutions were organized in such a way to obviate women's autonomy.

In addition to these schemes which contained women economically, women's sexual mobility was also secondary to that of men. While the Moyne Commission and the JWF promoted stable monogamous unions, they implicitly allowed for men to keep "outside women." While women were admonished to stay at home and remain faithful to their husbands, men were free to sow their seeds far and wide. In spite of promiscuity on the part of married men, it was women who were blamed for the problems of fatherless households. Instead of devising reforms that would affect poor families in meaningful ways, the Moyne Commission placed the problems of society on "the family", or the absence thereof.

It seems more than coincidental that in 1965 the Moynihan Report (U.S. Department of Labor 1965) suggested that the cause of social and economic ills among African Americans in the United States was fatherless homes. Families that are headed by female single parents continue to bear the brunt of accusations concerning the decline of African American males and African American society in general.

In Jamaica, with the official establishment of men as breadwinners, women's dependent status was also officially legitimated. The decline in female employment in all sectors of society during this period was an important consequence of this frontal attack on women's economic mobility and social independence. Sexist policies were in tandem with tactics which continued to marginalize the masses of poor people. This was in keeping with the social and political-economic status of people of African descent in all parts of the Caribbean and served as the linchpin of European development and the underdevelopment of Diaspora Africans. The influx of foreign capital into Jamaica along with conservative leadership reinforced the condition of the working class and unemployed in general and led to the superexploitation of women.

Labor Unions and Party Politics

An amalgam of political conflicts between Alexander Bustamante and Norman Manley, constitutional reform, and a gradualist approach to decolonization characterized the years following the 1938 rebellion. Bustamante and Manley fashioned themselves as advocates for the working class while at the same time they upheld the economic and political structures that benefitted the upper classes. While Bustamante and Manley were successful in quelling the conflict between capital and labor, they did so by mollifying working class insurgents and imploring them to work within the system.

Manley's paternalistic attitude was evident in a speech he gave to the striking workers in St. Mary on 2 June.

> My head is wiser than yours tonight and if we can stop disorder breaking out in Jamaica today and if we can sit down to tackle the bigger problems and time—supported by your loyalty and good behavior which is being watched all over the world—time will shew we have not fought in vain and it will be a better Jamaica. Place faith, hope and trust in the people who are trying to help you (Daily Gleaner 1938:19).

Thus, Manley admonished workers to behave—a strategy that ensured European and mulatto control over the means of production. Workers were also encouraged to think only in terms of selling their labor for a wage leaving them in much the same predicament they were in before the rebellion. Bustamante, who had gained a significantly larger following among the workers than Manley, also advocated for change that in essence was no change at all.

> The moment disorder starts we cannot help you. If you will only keep orderly and take a little increase today and probably a little raise in the next three or six months you will no doubt be better off and we will be able to do greater things, but so long as these strikes continue we will never be able to do greater things for you. We will not have the time and strength to do it (Daily Gleaner 1938: 19).

In spite of his conservative rhetoric, Bustamante gained the favor of the majority of workers. This allegiance was partially due to his arrest in the process of trying to effect a settlement between the workers and the colonial government. Moreover, he continually championed himself as a man of the people while at the same time representing Manley as a tool of the capitalists. These factors, in addition to his charisma and rhetorical gifts, gained him adulation among the working class. Bustamante used the occasion of the 1938 strikes to form labor unions under the title of the Bustamante Industrial Trade Unions. The name of the Union is indicative of his flair and narcissism as well as the degree of control he exercised within these organizations.

While Bustamante was busy controlling trade unionism, Manley established the People's National Party (PNP) on 18 September 1938. Bustamante became apprehensive regarding Manley's rise to prominence and feared that Manley was attempting to usurp his power among the working classes. Dissension between the two leaders escalated when Manley worked with colonial forces to democratize the B.I.T.U. and Bustamante railed against socialist elements within the PNP. In September 1940, when

Bustamante began serving a second jail sentence for violating wartime regulations, the PNP took control of the B.I.T.U. Upon Bustamante's release, his skirmishes with Manley resumed.

Bustamante's personal and ideological differences with Manley led him to form the Jamaica Labor Party (JLP) in July 1943. He led the JLP in much the same way that he did the B.I.T.U.—like a dictator. He shaped policy single-handedly and selected those candidates who were willing to follow his lead. Unlike the PNP, which espoused a program of "industrial development, public ownership of utilities,... [and] improved welfare services" (Kaufman 1985:48), the JLP did not have a well formulated program and served mostly as the electoral body for the B.I.T.U. While the PNP and JLP may have differed ideologically and organizationally, they had in common that each was controlled by middle class, mulatto leadership, each had a trade union and working class support, and each wielded power and influence in controlling voting behavior through patronage among the voting electorate.

During this early period of party formation, London was in the throes of devising constitutional reform for the island (see Munroe 1972). In 1944 the colonial government issued its constitution which granted universal adult suffrage. This may have appeared like a move toward a more democratic government when, in fact, it was not since the constitution continued to limit membership in the national legislature and Europeans maintained their authority over the colony. Peasant resistance and radical leftist movements were quickly suppressed as colonial officials squashed any attempts to subvert its power. The Rastafarian movement, which posed an ideological threat to the colonial regime, was harassed and kept under watchful surveillance.

RastafarI Initiatives

While Rastafarians as a group did not participate in the 1938 Rebellion, their anti-colonial rhetoric, which was couched in racial terms, was gaining influence among the disenfranchised. Leonard Howell attracted recruits at the Pinnacle where adherents numbered between five hundred to sixteen hundred. Daily life in this commune was redolent of maroon societies in that Rastas planted cash crops and engaged in polygyny, and Leonard Howell served as the African chief. Howell firmly believed in his greatness which was exemplified by his demanding taxes from his neighbors, who quickly reported him to local authorities. The police raided the community, but Howell escaped. He was soon captured and convicted for assaulting non-Rastas in the community and was jailed for a second two-year term on July 25, 1941.

After his release, Howell spent thirteen years in the United States. Upon his return to Jamaica, he reestablished the Pinnacle in 1953. Pinnacle residents resumed operations which included growing *ganja* and letting their hair grow into locks. Howell's group continued to harass neighbors and to preach violence. As a result, in 1954 the police destroyed the Pinnacle and forced its members to disperse to a slum area known as "Back-O-Wall" in Kingston. Howell, by this time advanced in age, claimed that he was god, changed his name to Gagunju Mahraj (or Gong), and consequently was committed to a mental institution.

Though the leadership was contained and the followers dispersed, the Rastafarian spirit was not dead. Rastas continued wearing dreadlocks, smoking *ganja*, and lambasting the Jamaican government (now referred to by Rastas as Babylon). In 1958, a mass meeting or *Grounation* of more than 300 Rastafarians attracted national attention. In the same year, a more radical branch of Rastas attempted to capture the city of Kingston. This aborted takeover resulted in the arrest of the incendiary group and the harassment of Rastas in general who were now considered a serious threat to the Jamaican authorities.

Another Rasta leader who was intent on destroying the colonial powers in Jamaica was Claudius Henry. Henry began to preach Rasta ideology in the 1930s. In an attempt to snuff out his anti-colonial rhetoric, he was arrested for preaching without a permit. In 1953 he was ordained as a minister in the United States and returned to Jamaica in 1957 to resume his campaign against European hegemony. He established his African Reform Church in Kingston and fashioned himself as the "Repairer of the Breach" and the "Moses of the Blacks." Like Howell before him, he began a campaign to encourage Jamaicans to return to Africa.

Henry sold tickets at one shilling each which read:

> Pioneering Israel's scattered children of African Origin "back home to Africa." This year 1959, deadline date—Oct. 5th; this new government is God's Righteous Kingdom of Everlasting Peace on Earth. "Creation's Second Birth." Holder of this Certificate is requested to visit the Headquarters at 18 Rosalie Avenue...August 1st, 1959, for our Emancipation Jubilee, commencing 9 A.M. sharp. Please reserve this Certificate for removal. No passport will be necessary for those returning to Africa, etc. We sincerely, "The Seventh Emmanuel's Brethren" fathering Israel's scattered and anointed prophet, Rev. C. V. Henry, R. B.
>
> Given this 2nd day of March 1959, in the year of the reign of His Imperial Majesty, 1st Emperor of Ethiopia, "God's Elect" Haile Selassie, King of Kings and Lord of Lords, Israel's Returned Messiah (Barrett 1977:96).

Henry's rhetoric, although couched in religious terms, constituted a political message that called for a new social order. Henry proposed that the only path that would lead the poor working class out of "destruction and captivity" was the exercise of their own agency (*Daily Gleaner* 1960:5).

He distributed thousands of pamphlets on the streets of Kingston that appealed to the poor and disenfranchised. In 1959, one of his messages read

> Dear Readers, should we at this time sacrifice such a righteous Government, for Jamaican Self-Government, or an other Self-Government, in the world?...shall we sacrifice the continent of Africa for the island of Jamaica? Shall we refuse God's offer for repatriation back home to Africa and a life of everlasting peace and freedom, with Him under our own vine and fig tree, and go back into slavery, under these wicked, unrighteous and oppressive rulers of Jamaica? God forbid (*Daily Gleaner* 1960:5).

Because many Jamaicans were living in impoverished conditions and because they were already steeped in Christian ideology that made frequent references to Egypt and Ethiopia, the climate was ripe for the reception of Henry's call. Although Henry later claimed that the proposed meeting date was not to repatriate Jamaicans to Africa, but only to discuss the possibility with government officials in an open meeting, hundreds of believers sold their land and other property with the hopes of returning to the promised land. Henry was admonished to cease these repatriation activities for one year and was fined £100. In spite of these repressive tactics, Henry blamed the Prime Minister, Norman Manley, for failing to assist in repatriating Jamaicans to Africa.

> Henry is reported to have told his congregation that if they did not get to leave Jamaica back to Africa, they should take off his [Manley's"] head and kick it up Rosalie Avenue like [a] football (Daily Gleaner 1960:5).

Predictably, the police stepped up their suppression of the African Reform Church and other Rastafarian communities. On 6 April 1960 Henry's Kingston headquarters was raided and a cache of armaments, ammunition, and marijuana was uncovered. The police made similar findings in tributaries in Clarendon. This threat of armed insurrection was unusual for Rastafarians at the time and for any time hence.

Henry's group and other rebellious Rastafarians roused fear in the hearts of many Jamaican citizens, but called attention to the disenfranchisement of poor people. In spite of these initiatives, they were unable to sustain a concerted force against the colonial regime.

Rastas and the Rise of International Capital

The influx of foreign capital exacerbated the woes of working class Jamaicans. Beginning in the 1950's North American and Canadian capital accelerated the process of uneven development. Alcoa, Alcan, and Pichiney Ugine Kuhmann were leaders[3] in making Jamaica the largest producer of bauxite ore in the late 1950s and 1960s. By 1980 Jamaica was the major supplier of bauxite to the United States. Reynolds and Kaiser accelerated bauxite production, replacing sugar as the island's primary export. At its height, the mining sector represented over two-thirds of all exports. The incursion of these companies into Jamaica was typical of international capitalism in that raw materials were extracted from the Third World then processed and commodified in First World nations. Only a small sector of the Jamaican population reaped any gains from the presence of these companies.

Bauxite/alumina workers in Jamaica made more than twice the wage of workers in other sectors of the economy; however, this wage was far below that of aluminum workers in the United States (Kaufman 1985:31). Deleterious effects on the Jamaican economy at large were numerous. As an example, the increase in wages to bauxite workers encouraged an increase in prices for basic commodities and the consumption of imported luxury items. Moreover,

> The companies owned 14% of the island [calculated from Manley 1974:259] and a considerably higher percentage of cultivable land. This aggravated the breakdown of rural society, encouraged urban migration, pushed up land prices, led to environmental problems, and accelerated the concentration of land holdings [Tramm 1977; Stone 1975:4] (Kaufman 1985:30–31).

While capital was heavily invested in mining and manufacturing industries, high unemployment rates among the working class continued. Moreover, along with increased mechanization, the demand for agricultural laborers decreased. The local and foreign elite were secure in their position since the unemployed served as a reserve army of potential labor which precluded workers from organizing a viable campaign for higher wages. All of these factors combined to reduce wages and replicate the class structure of a slave society. Moreoever, class lines continued to parallel color lines since the elite and middle class were synonymous with lighter skin, while poverty was tantamount to being darker skinned.

The mulatto leadership of the newly formed PNP and JLP embraced the cultural and political presence of the British empire. As such, national identity during the transition period to independence did not represent the cultural or economic needs of the African Jamaican populace. The conservative rhetoric of both political parties instigated the anti-capitalist

---

3. In addition to these leading aluminum manufacturers, Kaiser Aluminum and Chemical Corporation, Reynolds Metals Company, and Swiss Aluminum (Alusuisse) contributed to the extraction of Jamaican bauxite (Kaufman 1985:25).

rhetoric espoused by Rastafarians. Even though Rastas constituted a counterforce to Manley's and Bustamante's accommodationist approach, Claudius Henry's plans for armed struggle notwithstanding, their advocacy of African Jamaican rule was submerged under a litany of religious and repatriation bravado.

The fact that RastafarI protest was couched in religious terms was not new to Jamaica since, as we saw in the previous chapter, movements in the eighteenth and nineteenth centuries were spurred by religious injunctions. As was the case with Baptist leaders of the preceding century, Rastafarian religious ideology was diametrically opposed to colonial power. Moving beyond the incantations of Pukkamina and Obeah, RastafarI preached condemnation of Babylon (the western capitalist world) and advocated repatriation for the masses of African Jamaicans.

In spite of their lack of political organization, Rastafarians continued to preach the gospel of African identity and race consciousness to the poor and disenfranchised, and posed a serious ideological threat to the colonial order. Along with the doctrine of African repatriation, the promulgation of Haile Selassie as a "Black God" also called into question the primacy of the English royalty, and by association, European colonial rule on the island. RastafarI's relentless racial chauvinism led the colonial government to employ a series of physically repressive tactics against them. This repression continued throughout the 1960s until Rasta were mollified into a more pacifist organization.

Meanwhile the bourgeoisie and elite were consolidating their power and promoting a philosophy which depicted Jamaican society as politically, culturally, and racially harmonious. This mystification was encapsulated in a single phrase, "Out of many, One People" (Richardson 1983:143–167) which continues to be used to represent Jamaica's public image. This fiction was created in order to mount a counter ideology to Rastas' race-conscious agenda and other oppositional forces. The government was bent on sending a message to international corporations that the island was safe for foreign capitalist investment. Alexander Bustamante was especially skillful in painting a picture of racial harmony in the national press.

> People in the world have come to point at Jamaica as a leading example—as a small country where reason, law and order are fundamental to the country and our people, and where races work and live in harmony with ever increasing respect for each other, and capital therefore has regarded us as a safe place to come while local capital gained faith to join in doing their part in our development (*Daily Gleaner* 1960:10).

Manley and Bustamante continued to speak of the common interests of labor and capital; however, this hyperbole masked the maldistribution of income and the social stratification that characterized the island. Jamaica, indeed, provided a "safe place" for foreign and local capitalists, but not for the average working class Jamaican. The accumulation of wealth by the upper classes was paralleled by a deepening poverty among the masses. Not only did unemployment increase and low wages persist, but medical services and educational opportunities dwindled while the rich continued to build larger mansions far away from the congested yards of poor people.

During the late 1950s and early 1960s some Rastafarians believed that real change would only come about as the result of armed insurrection. At the same time Claudius Henry was amassing his cache of arms, his son Ronald was leading a cadre of Jamaicans and African Americans in guerrilla warfare. This band was summarily rounded up and arrested and Ronald Henry was killed by police. Even though these violent forces were subdued, a more general movement from within Jamaica and from the Black Power movement in the United States constituted a potential threat to the hegemony of the elite.[4]

While Henry's group constituted the most radical arm of the early Rastafarian movement, other Rastas were engaged in forging a new image of themselves. With the help of a group of university professors, they sought to carve out an image which maintained their Afrocentric perspective by emphasizing the need to "return" to Africa, but one which also depicted them as peaceful advocates of a back-to-Africa philosophy. Toward these ends Rastafarian Mortimo Planno approached members of the faculty at the University of the West Indies (UWI Mona campus) and requested that a study be undertaken to show the non-violent aspects of the organization.

This group of university professors, led by Rex Nettleford, M.G. Smith, and Roy Augier, conducted research for two weeks. Through this research they outlined the political and economic conditions which gave rise to RastafarI and spelled out the doctrine of the movement. They also laid out a plan of "rehabilitation" that was accepted by some Rastas, but "rejected out of hand by the Niabinghi militants" (Nettleford 1970:44).

The Committee recommended building low cost housing, the extension of water, electricity, and other public amenities to squatter settlements, as well as technical instruction for youth at civic centers in Kingston. The Committee also recommended that a branch of the Ethiopian Orthodox

---

4. The colonial regime used a number of repressive measures to prevent African American Black nationalism from entering Jamaica. In 1960 a group of African Americans called the "First Africa Corps, Sons and Daughters of Africa" were prevented from entering the island (*Daily Gleaner* 1960:1). Throughout the 1960s the government barred literature by Malcolm X and Stokely Carmichael (aka Kwame Ture).

Church in Western Kingston move into areas accessible to a larger sector of poor Rasta adherents. The rationale for these proposals was to "rehabilitate Rastas into the wider society" (Ibid:44).

The committee laid out a list of ten recommendations (see Appendix B) that was presented to the government, then headed by Norman Manley. The government heeded several of these suggestions including the proposition that Rastas receive assistance in repatriating to Africa. In 1961, the government sent a small mission to Africa which consisted of three Rastafarians and six other representatives. The entourage spent nine weeks touring Sierra Leone, Liberia, Nigeria, Ghana, and Ethiopia. During their nine day visit to Ethiopia, Haile Selassie, who had already set aside land for Diaspora Africans in Shashemene, clearly asserted that he was not interested in unskilled workers migrating to his country (Faith 1990:301–302).

Many middle class Jamaicans were unhappy that the government was spending their tax dollars to deal with Rastafarian issues, which, in their opinion, were anathema to Jamaica as a whole. However, others began to express support for the organization and several lawyers, teachers, and other professionals joined the movement. Middle class youth also began to exhibit Rasta symbolism in protest against parental authority.

When the island gained its independence in 1962, Rastafarians had none of the fervor of the groups led by Howell or Henry. Some even indicated their faith in the political structure by running for political office (Gray 1991:259n; Morrish 1982:78–79). Nevertheless, Rastafari continued to exhibit racial pride and espouse an African identity—two factors that distinguished them from other oppositional groups. The mulatto political elites responded to Rastafari rhetoric by reinterpreting calls for racial self-determination as the promulgation of race hatred. Norman Manley and Alexander Bustamante called for racial harmony—a laudable goal if only it had been based in reality. Instead, political leaders invited the incursion of more foreign capital and capital intensification which further marginalized the poor—mostly dark skinned Jamaicans—while at the same time speaking of racial bias as a thing of the past (Gray 1991:56). Even though Rastafarians constituted one of the strongest avant garde groups of the time, they did not engage in direct confrontation with the political-economic structure.

> For Rastafarians, oppression in Jamaica called for a studied retreat and disengagement. Furthermore, unfolding events demanded constant study and analysis, and this entailed meditation, discussion, and reading the bible, seeking for answers.... to belong to this culture of resistance, enlistees had to meet the rigorous intellectual demands of the Rastafarian community and remain faithful to the idea of repatriation. It is at this point that

the differences between Rastafarians and the rebellious youths become obvious (Gray 1991:74).

In addition to Rastafarians, the New World Group, the Unemployed Workers' Council, and the Young Socialist League organized to combat uneven development and colonial rule. These organizations emerged at a time when youths were exerting their lawlessness, and university intellectuals were demanding their right to criticize the government as part of their intellectual freedom. The New World Group was established in 1962 as a study group for these intellectuals, and their journal, the *New World Quarterly*, served as a vehicle for expressing their opinions on the problems confronting the region. Each of these organizations had in common their displeasure with the JLP-led government, but ideological differences regarding strategies and desired outcomes created dissension within and among these groups.

Members of the New World Group, the Unemployed Workers, and the Young Socialists were at odds with RastafarI's back-to-Africa agenda nor its emphasis on religious resolutions to class conflict. According to Gray (1991:144–152) the schism between Rasta ideology and that of other oppositional groups was that the former was mired in race and the latter in class. Notwithstanding the fact that race and class had always been intimately connected in African/European relations, these groups could not find a common ground. Non-Rasta groups were wedded to the idea of agency and participation in the political process. In contrast, the agency of Rastafarians, with few exceptions, "was tempered by the belief that unfolding political events represented divinely ordained plans" (Ibid:148). In spite of their competing ideologies, all of these groups were influenced by global Black nationalist and pan-African movements that were the hallmark of the decade.

The 1960s were characterized by movements for independence and self-determination in Africa and the African Diaspora. Black nationalist groups such as the Black Panthers, the Republic of New Africa, and the Organization of African American Unity were capturing the imagination of the masses of poor people in the United States and other regions. Kwame Ture (formerly Stokely Carmichael) picked up the gauntlet from Marcus Garvey and Kwame Nkrumah in formulating his All African People's Revolutionary Party. From this platform, Toure advocated repatriation and self-determination under the banner of "Africa for Africans." Even though the Jamaican government banned Toure's work as well as other literature that they considered incendiary, the proximity of Jamaica to the United States made the enforcement of these laws impossible. The pan-African ethos that characterized the 1960s heightened the reception of Emperor Haile Selassie on his visit to Jamaica in 1966.

People travelled from all parts of Jamaica to see the Emperor, who was overwhelmed by the throngs who had come

> from all parts of Jamaica, coming on foot, in cars, in drays, in carts, in hired buses, on bicycles and by every means of transport that can be imagined, and there never has been in the whole history of Jamaica such a spontaneous, heart-warming and sincere welcome to any person, whether visiting monarch, visiting V.I.P. or returning leader of any Jamaican party (Owens 1976:250)

The emperor's visit broadened the acceptance of Rasta in Jamaica that had already begun with the UWI study. Police stopped their harassment of the group, did not make arrests for *ganja* smoking, and some members of the middle class and elite demonstrated an attachment to Rasta and attempted to be on friendly terms with them (Chevannes 1990:75). Another critical series of events that influenced the acceptance of Rastafarians revolved around the radical ideology of Walter Rodney (1942–1980).

Walter Rodney, a Guyanese scholar-activist, was a pivotal figure in the ideological development of race and class consciousness in Jamaica in the late 1960s. He was a lecturer at the University of the West Indies (Mona campus) and an enigma among university professors, given his emphasis on teaching African history and its connection with contemporary events in the Diaspora. He also differed from the UWI intelligentsia, youth organizations, and Rastafarians in that he sought to politicize the Jamaican masses and did not limit himself to the constraints of the ivory tower. In some ways, Rodney's ideology resonated with that of Rastafarians in emphasizing the importance of learning African history as part of the Jamaican struggle for liberation. Unfortunately, he was also like Rastas in his lack of attention to women's status in Jamaican society.

Even his well-known and much celebrated treatise on racism and colonialism, *The Groundings with my Brothers* (1990), does not address the problem of sexism. Indeed, the title of this text, which emphasizes his alliance with his "brothers", totally ignores women's subordinate position throughout Africa and Diaspora. Nevertheless, Rodney became a dangerous figure in the eyes of the newly independent country given his appeal to university students and his direct and ideological connection with working class people in the Kingston slums.

This was a significant development in Jamaica since other groups who were advocating for change, for example, the New World Group, did not seek contact with the general populace and remained theoretical in focus. Even from a theoretical perspective these groups did not directly criticize the Jamaican government.

Rodney's message was given more weight as a result of events in the United States. In April 1968 race relations exploded when Martin Luther

King, Jr. was assassinated and Black Power became the rallying cry of a large sector of poor African Americans. Rodney drew on this historical moment to underscore the necessity for violence in fighting global racial inequitites. His message was compelling, but many Jamaican enthusiasts rejected his stance on violence. Rodney defended his position by emphasizing the difference in violence for the sake of oppression and violence for the sake of equality. He insisted that

> violence aimed at the recovery of human dignity and at equality cannot be judged by the same yardstick as violence aimed at the maintenance of discrimination and oppression (Rodney 1990:22).

It was not long before the authorities tried to oust Rodney from the University. His threat to the status quo was clearly based on his assertion that power in the hands of African Jamaicans signified an end to imperialism which, by historical definition, meant an end to White and mulatto rule. He advocated power for the masses of people in the Caribbean coupled with a revitalization of African culture (Ibid 28). Rodney's message struck at the heart of uneven development in Jamaica in so far as it pointed to the ways in which race paralleled class, a central theme in his classic work, *How Europe Underdeveloped Africa* (1972). This treatise on the European invasion and exploitation of Africa emphasized the inverse nature between European and African development. The development of European societies, based on their plunder of Africa, was directly (and intentionally) related to the underdevelopment of Africa. Moreover, Rodney emphasized the political and cultural commonality of all people of African descent in the Diaspora and was unequivocal as to the solution to this problem.

Failing to find legal grounds to expel Rodney from the UWI, the government, then headed by JLP leader Hugh Shearer, seized the opportunity to prevent him from disembarking from an airplane upon his return from a Black Writer's Conference in Montreal, Canada. Jamaica's elitism and commitment to imperialism was matched in Rodney's home country, Guyana, where he was killed by a fire bomb in 1980.

Neither Rastafarians nor any of the other Black consciousness groups in Jamaica had the fervor or political grounding of Walter Rodney; however, these groups continued to express their resentment over the economic control held by the mulatto elite. University intellectuals, many of them members of the New World Group and the Young Socialist League, attempted to continue Rodney's activism in the form of an alternative press. There was much debate over the aims and objectives of the press, given that there were elements who favored merely engendering discussion over national issues

---

5. For a detailed discussion of the New World Group and its literary organ, *Abeng*, see Gray (1991:166–182).

and those who were prepared to continue Walter Rodney's imperative. In the final analysis the latter element won the day and began publication of *Abeng*, a weekly newspaper, on 1 February 1969.[5]

In the beginning *Abeng* addressed issues of poverty, housing, police brutality and disenfranchisement, and emphasized the racial character of this marginalization. Their attention to these issues was heavily influenced by African and Black nationalist movements in the United States and Africa. In an effort to conform to Rodney's injunctions, *Abeng* gave Rastafarians and unemployed people space to vent their views (Gray 1991:172). In addition, Marcus Garvey, Jr. was an important voice that greatly influenced the ideological orientation of the group.

Not parenthetically, the language used in *Abeng* couched its proclamations in male terms, such as "[B]lack man time come." As will be evident in the following chapters, the male tone of the organization was indicative of the Jamaican definition of liberation which was tantamount to "male" liberation. At some point in its short life, *Abeng* became aware of their male bias and printed a position statement on women's marginalized status.

Abeng stands for complete liberation of the female in our society. ABENG believes:

1) that women are not sexual objects…They are whole complete human beings. Women's bodies are not commodities for cheap shows and cheap pleasure.
2) Women must be free to develop their mental and other capabilities to the fullest not only for their well-being but for also the well being of the country.
3) Women must get equal pay for equal work.
4) Large groups of women work in deplorable conditions. This must stop. Some domestic workers get as little as £2.0 per week or even less. Many of these women have children to support. There should be a domestic worker's union. Nurses too also work under bad conditions and are poorly paid. Bus conductresses are given a difficult time and are used by the system to police the people. This is a good example of how black people are used against one another.
5) Economic hardship makes it necessary for most mothers to work. Under these circumstances we believe it is only fair that men should share the burden of housework and child rearing.
6) Women have a right to take full part in political activities and should be proportionately represented in the Government of their lives. We note that there is not a single female minister of Government in Jamaica.
7) The education of girls should be radically altered. Women must organize unions to protect their rights which were guaranteed by the bill of Human Rights and by the constitution of Jamaica.

2

8)   We suggest that all our readers who feel sympathy for the plight
     of women in this country, write and tell us what you think can
     be done. We are ready to co-operate in forming a group with oth-
     ers to bring aid to unmarried mothers (Abeng 1969:2).

This insertion stands out in the *Abeng* annals due to its rarity in the
publication itself and in Diaspora African movements in general.

The failure to more aggressively address the issue of sexism in Jamaica is
a significant fault. To add to this deficiency various antagonistic strands soon
developed within the *Abeng* group. Marxists drew attention to the collusion
of the local and foreign elite in dominating the working class, but failed to suggest alternatives to this capitalistic structure. Moreover, the group as a whole
was steadfast in its critique of the status quo, but was unable to mount a plan
for structural economic and political change. One of the primary reasons for
this was that Black Power advocates saw Jamaica's problems *only* in terms of
race. The Marxists were just as myopic in their narrowly class based agendas.

Marcus Garvey, Jr. was of the former ilk and proclaimed that race was
the only rallying point, that Black was Black, whether rich or poor (*Abeng*
1969:20). Unfortunately, this body that drew so much energy from Walter Rodney could not come to terms with his basic philosophy, that class
privilege was based on racial hegemony. Moreover, even while the Marxists as a group were advocating a class ideology, their middle class education had distanced them from the lumpenproleteriat. This was evidenced
by their refusal to allow Rastafarian leader Claudius Henry into the *Abeng*
group (Gray 1991:181). Young Rastafarians in the group pointed out the
class differences within the organization and the contradiction of class
privileges while they advocated for radicalism among the working class
(Ibid:175).

Large sectors of the working class were illiterate, therefore they were
unable to partake in the newspaper's debates, unstructured as they were.
Disharmony within *Abeng*, coupled with their lack of dialogue with the
masses of laborers and the unemployed, led to the organization's demise
only ten months after its inception.

Abeng activists rechanneled their energies into trade union movements
and student protests (Ibid:183). This period also marked the attenuation
of any significant political activity on the part of Rastafarians. In its place,
Rasta began to promote a "peace and love" philosophy which caught the
attention of middle class youth. These youth either joined the movement
or began to mimic Rastafarian symbolic expressions without embracing
its religious beliefs.

Meanwhile the growing infiltration of foreign businesses increased the
level of discontent among the working class. Continued government repression of Black consciousness and Marxist oppositional forces, unemployment, and injustices in the judicial system combined to fuel disaffection

among the masses. A major crisis in sugar production also added to the JLP's crumbling reputation (Girvan and Jefferson 1971:37–54).

The reformulated People's National Party seized this opportunity to reclaim allegiance from the laboring masses and to feign an attachment to RastafarI. Michael Manley opportunistically used a cane ostensibly presented to him by Haile Selassie during his visit to Jamaica in 1966. He named his cane the "rod of redemption" which led many to believe that the rod had supernatural powers. He also appealed to the working class masses by incorporating reggae tunes into his campaign (Kaufman 1985:71–72). By manipulating the artifacts of popular culture, Manley captured Rastafarian allegiance and the religious imagination of the majority of the Jamaican populace.

While Manley's intentions may have been strategic, his sincerity is difficult to imagine given that the party remained dominated by mulatto bourgeoisie and elite classes. Manley's rise to power in 1972 was characterized by a number of reforms which ostensibly were instituted to redistribute the national income but not to eliminate the class structure. A levy was placed on the foreign owned bauxite corporations and other strategies were employed to nationalize the economy. In addition to these issues, Manley made the inexorable mistake of developing an alliance with Cuba.

This, added to his democratic socialist rhetoric, alienated local capitalists and foreign interests. Given the central place held by the United States within the International Monetary Fund (IMF) and its antipathy for Castro's Cuba, Manley's new alliance did not set well with the U.S. government. With the help of the JLP opposition, foreign and local elites reacted to these attempts at resource redistribution by launching a campaign to destabilize the PNP and ultimately oust it from power. Tourism was discouraged by the American press which wreaked havoc on Jamaica's second largest foreign exchange earner. In addition, many businesses left the island and international banks refused to extend loans to the Jamaican government (Harrison 1988:105).

These coercive tactics forced the PNP to seek aid from the International Monetary Fund, whose austere policies exacerbated the conditions of poor people and heightened party conflicts. With few international resources that were not controlled by the IMF, Manley found himself unable to put his populist agenda into action. The Jamaican government provided incentives for foreign investors and developed an infrastructure to service the tourist industry. These investments benefitted local and foreign elites, but did little to effect the economy as a whole since most of the supplies used by tourist concerns, such as furniture, food, and transport vehicles were imported. Moreover, tourism was the bane of the masses since it acted to raise the prices of most goods and services, placing them out of the reach of poor people.

The masses of people were stuck, as they had been since the end of slavery, with only their labor to sell—and that at horrendously low prices. Others, such as small peasants, continued to eke out a subsistence living without the assistance of lending agencies which favored larger businesses when giving loans and credits. The other sector of poor people were petty traders who got by, legally or otherwise, as best they could.

People who constitute this "informal sector" engage in a myriad of activities that allow them to circumvent taxes, licenses, sanitary laws, and other regulations that are customarily assumed by the formal sector. Examples of occupations include street vending of perishable or non-perishable items, mechanical repair, and an assortment of illegal activities including prostitution, gambling, and drugs. In the 1970s *ganja* was the mainstay of the Jamaican economy (Newsweek 1980:86).

Not surprisingly, the majority of people who participate in the "informal sector" were (and are) women. In the 1970s women experienced twice the unemployment as men. Because men had more saleable skills, such as construction or automechanical competence, they also had greater access than women to more lucrative occupations. In a sample studied by Harrison (1988) in the 1970s 33% of the women were engaged in some kind of domestic service and 26% "in general services (e.g., casual street cleaning, hairstyling, and spiritual healing). In contrast, 40% of the men in the sample were engaged in general services (e.g, taxi-driving, vehicle repair, and photography") (Ibid:106–107) which allowed them to make higher wages. Women's labor as domestics, street vendors, and other relatively low paying jobs was, and continues to be, exacerbated by their responsibilities as heads of households and caretakers of children and elderly relatives.

Even though many of the products sold in the informal sector are made in the home, other products are manufactured by the formal sector and distributed to people in the informal sector for marketing. This arrangement primarily benefits capitalist firms who avoid setting up or expanding retail stores. Even though small scale entrepreneurs enjoy some measure of autonomy in terms of controlling the marketing of these products, they remain dependent on capital for their survival. Capital intensification promoted by the JLP only exacerbated this state of affairs.

The deteriorated state of the Jamaican economy led to overwhelming support for the JLP who won a sweeping victory on 31 October 1980. The leader of the party was Syrian born and Harvard educated Edward Seaga who formerly served as Minister of Development and Minister of Finance and Planning from 1962 to 1972. Contrary to Manley's democratic socialist appeal, Seaga's revitalization program promoted free enterprise for local capitalists and an increase in foreign investment.

Seaga negotiated massive loans from the IMF which Jamaica had little chance of repaying. At the same time, the IMF resumed its austerity measures which included the proliferation of international corporate control of the island. While profits flooded into foreign coffers, unemployment reached 35% in 1980 with especially deleterious affects on young people and women (Harrison 1988:106). International enterprises gained a strangle hold on the Jamaican people as unemployment was matched by a deterioration of services. The Caribbean Basin Initiative (CBI) engineered by U.S. President Ronald Reagan further peripheralized poor people. While profits were returned to foreign investors, none of this windfall trickled down to the masses of Jamaicans. Within a short period of time Jamaica's dependency status was exacerbated, as capital intensive industry renewed hard times.

The uneven development of Jamaican society in the 1970s and 1980s gave rise to yet another wave of emigration to the U.S., Canada, and England. Many of those who remained, especially peasants who were pushed off their land, and other wage laborers, were

> absorbed into the urban informal economic sector, which encompasses income-producing activities outside formal sector wages, pensions, and gratuities (Ibid:107).

What Rastas called the "brown-man"[6] government pursued a course of "industrialization by invitation" which focused on capital intensive inputs and ignored the possibilities of land redistribution and agricultural development that could have benefitted the masses of Jamaican people. Even with the election of P. J. Patterson in 1991, the first dark-skinned person to hold the post of Prime Minister in the history of the island, capital intensification continued forcing many people out of work and into the informal sector or into the ranks of the unemployed.

Pattterson's policies have basically been a rehashing of the old practices. His formula for economic recovery relied (and continues to rely) on foreign capital and investment as a way to alleviate rising unemployment rates and the ever increasing national debt (Scott and Lewis 1992:22). During his regime unemployment continued to hover around 25%, with rates for women twice as high as men. Housing is at a premium leaving many people homeless or forced to set up squatter communities. Sanitation is abysmal in Kingston, the capital city, which in many areas resem-

---

6. Rastas and other Jamaicans refer to mulattoes and other light skinned people as "brown men." I choose not to reify this term here since from a broader perspective it can be misunderstood as all brown men of African descent. I wish to make a distinction between brown men and those people who are actually mulattoes or descendants thereof, and who enjoy economic and cultural privilege in Jamaica based on their skin color and their economic advantage.

bles a war torn zone. Transportation is atrocious. People are crammed into buses like slaves on a slave ship. From one year to the next these conditions deteriorate and give rise to increased tensions that implode among the masses of poor people.

At the same time, under the guise of development, Structural Adjustment Programs exact a number of hardships on poor people. Small farmers are unable to produce sufficient food for local consumption given inflated costs of fertilizer and tools which gives rise to increased food importation. Services for the urban poor are also reduced especially in the areas of education, health, and nutrition. Thus, structural adjustment has not meant development that benefits the masses of poor people, but adjustment that once again alters their lives to bear the burden for local and international elite (McAfee 1991:68–69).

While Rastafarians have long railed against the capitalist economy, they have not actively worked toward its demise. Like other Jamaicans, they are dependent on the capitalist structure for survival. This includes self-employed Rastas who sell brooms and arts and crafts and well-to-do Rastas who sell reggae on the international market. Rastafarians will remain part of the capitalist system as long as the means of production is in the hands of a small elite class.

Chapter 4

Women and the Rise of RastafarI

Rastafarian scholars have outlined the basic principles of RastafarI which include the belief in the divinity of Haile Selassie, that *ganja* is a holy herb, and that repatriation is the salvation of African descended people. Although some of the more recent literature (Chevannes 1995:121–124 *passim;* Lake 1994; Ray 1997; Rowe 1985) includes the tenet that Rasta women are subordinate to Rasta men, few have elaborated on this thesis. In spite of the outpouring of works on Rastafarians, it has only been in the 1980s and 1990s that scholars have begun to pay attention to the female aspect of the organization. Maureen Rowe, a Jamaican Rastafarian scholar, has written on the issue of male dominance from an internal perspective. My own work and that of Ray (1997) represents empirical research among Jamaican Rastafarian women (and secondarily from other Rastas in England).

Given Rasta's emphasis on liberation for African people world-wide, the existence of male dominance within the organization would lead one to wonder why and how this contradiction persists. I suggest that it persists for the same reason that sexism in other parts of Jamaica (and the world) endures—the unwillingness of men to relinquish their privilege and control over valuable resources. Cultural ideology is the answer to how unsubstantiated ideas about women become normative.

Many Rastas believe that a woman can only enter into RastafarI through Rasta men. Rastafarian women are said to receive guidance from Rasta men and are sometimes dependent on them to gain access to the organization. Rasta men are also considered the spiritual leaders of the movement and the heads of households. The Rastafarian phrase "to grow a dawta," which means to mentally, spiritually, and ideologically initiate women into RastafarI, underscores the child-like status ascribed to women. Men view women's minds as *tabula rasa*, or a blank state, upon which they must inscribe their wisdom and guidance. Although not all Rastafarian women abide by these guidelines, a large proportion do. Maureen Rowe explicates the patriarchal structure of the organization.

> There can be no denying the fact that RastafarI is a patriarchal movement. The male is at the head, having responsibility for conducting rituals, interpreting events of significance to the community, the care and protection of the family as well as the community. RastafarI is based on the

Bible, it therefore follows that its structure and philosophy would pattern that which unfolds in the Bible (Rowe 1985:13–14).

While Rowe concedes the patriarchal nature of RastafarI, she goes on to suggest that women who "sight RastafarI," even those who find some of the rules restrictive, "have...an attraction for this structured and disciplined way of life" (Ibid:16). While this may be the case, this observation raises more questions than it answers. Indeed, in talking with many sisters throughout the island, it did appear that the majority seemed reconciled to the Rastafarian code of behavior.

The Bible itself is a textual source which validates women's subordination, but a source that few Caribbean scholars challenge given the imbeddedness of Christianity, not only among Rastas, but among Jamaicans as a whole. Nevertheless, in the next chapter I address ways in which African and western religious ideology negatively impact on Rastafarian and other Jamaican women.

As Rowe (1985) asserts, there are other factors that tend to reinforce male superiority within the organization. The fact that RastafarI was organized by men and that men created its ideology makes its androcentric emphasis unremarkable. The fact that Leonard Howell and Claudius Henry considered themselves to be prophets, gods, or Jesus Christ reincarnated is telling. The current leader of the Bobo Shanti also considers himself, and is considered by his followers, to be a god.

Howell, one of the most pivotal leaders of the movement, labelled himself President General of the King of Kings Mission. He considered himself, and was considered by others, to be a prophet and was venerated as if he were a god. According to Hill (1983:35–36), after Howell set up the Pinnacle in 1940, he described himself as the returned messiah. Paul Earlington, a member of the EWF at the time, stated that Howell encouraged his followers to believe that "when you go to him, [it] is god you are talking to." (Ibid:36). That members of the Pinnacle worshipped him as a god is indicated in the following song they sang in his praises.

Leonard Howell seeks me and he finds me,
Fills my heart my glee;
That's why I am happy all the day,
For I know what Leonard Howell is doing for my soul,
That's why I am happy all the day.
(as quoted in Hill 1983:35)

The male centeredness of the movement, along with the fact that early Rastas were regarded as scruffy outcasts, acted to inhibit a greater female presence. According to government data (see Appendix C) there are 2,588 Rasta women and 10,574 Rasta men (0-44 years old) out of a total Jamaican population of 2.5 million. Austin-Broos (1987:21) explains the disparities between the numbers of women and men by suggesting that RastafarI

> has not been attractive to working class women with religious sensibility simply because its ethic, symbolism and social context, more often address the concerns of men.

The domination of women throughout the years has been so great, that lay people outside of Jamaica are often surprised when I tell them that there are Rastafarian women, since many believe that there are only male Rastas. While most of these comments come from people who only have a glimpse of Jamaica from the outside, this misconception is, nevertheless, grounded in the way in which Rasta has been promoted by Rastas themselves and by others.

The very symbolism of RastafarI is male. The male lion (see Figure 1) that represents RastafarI is indicative of the androcentric force of the organization. The maleness of the symbol is palpable and suggests dominance and aggressiveness, characteristics that are associated with males. The dreadlocks, even though worn by both women and men, are often worn by men in a style to mimic (and is referred to by men as) a lion's mane. The lion is also representative of Haile Selassie who used this symbol to represent the Conquering Lion of Judah.

The preponderance of male symbolism in Rasta art is particularly evident in Rasta sculpture. During a 1996 visit to Negril on the northeast coast of

Figure 1

the island, I noticed that many of the sculptors were beginning to include women in their works. This awareness that women should be included was almost refreshing. Unfortunately, the women were depicted as literal appendages of men—emerging out of the bodies of men and babies emerging out of women. There were no sculptures of women standing independently. Other areas of RastafarI culture also give primacy to the male especially music, language, religion, and dress. I will elaborate on these dimensions in the chapters below. At this juncture, a description of the major Rasta groups and how women are situated therein is instructive.

RastafarI Houses

Most Rastas are located in the St. Andrew/Kingston metropolitan area and consist of three main groups: the Twelve Tribes of Israel, the Nyabingi, and the Bobo Shanti. There are also Rastas who are not affiliated with any particular group. (An enumeration of other religious groups is given in Appendix D). Interestingly, the 1991 population census did not find it necessary to enumerate the number of Rastas as a separate group, but placed them within the category "Other" (Population Census 1991).

Each Rastafarian group is organized slightly differently and varies in terms of its perspectives regarding racial issues and their treatment of women. In the following sections I describe each of the major Rastafarian sects and ways that women are viewed.

The Twelve Tribes

RastafarI, on the whole, is an acephalous organization. There is no single leader of the entire group and no central organization. Twelve Tribes was founded in Trench Town in 1968 by Vernon Carrington, also known as Gad, a former higgler who sold herbal drinks from a push cart. In the Twelve Tribes' formative years, Carrington was a member of the Ethiopian World Federation and a Revivalist church. When he formed the organization, he held supreme authority. During my latest visit to Jamaica (August 1997), I learned that Gad still headed the Twelve Tribes but it was unclear whether he exercised the same degree of control.

Most other Rastas consider the Twelve Tribes to be the most hierarchical of all the sects. The original organization encompassed a ruling council which was under the direct control of Gad. Unlike other Rastafarian groups where decisions are made communally, Gad makes all of the important decisions and takes ultimate responsibility for the yard.

Twelve Tribes members also differ in their proscriptions regarding diet and dress. They advocate the wearing of dreadlocks, long skirts or dresses for women, and a vegetarian diet; however, if members choose not to strictly adhere to these rules, they are allowed freedom of choice. Nevertheless, all Twelve Tribes women practice the same dress codes as other Rasta women.

Initially, other Rastas looked disparagingly upon members of the Twelve Tribes because of their hierarchical, and in some cases, elitist structure. According to White (1984:294), the Twelve Tribes placed a great deal of emphasis on

> conversion, the various rigid dicta, and, most significant of all, the secret rites—all of this traditionally had been anathema to Rasta. To make matters worse, in the eyes of other Rastas, the Twelve Tribes were collecting money; believers were asked to pay twenty cents a week into a fund for repatriation.

The Twelve Tribes remained a cohesive group until the late 1980s when their headquarters on Hope Road was abandoned. However, the group is extant with members living in all parts of the island.

According to the literature and based on my observations, the Twelve Tribes and the Nyabingi are the largest groups, the former being more organized and more conservative than others. Following the UWI study in 1960, many middle class youths joined the movement, much to the dismay of their parents (van Dijk 1988). Even though the Twelve Tribes is known for having more middle class members than the other groups, poor Jamaicans constitute a large part of the organization.

Many Rastafarians profess that RastafarI is not a religion; however, a cursory look at the Twelve Tribes belies this notion. Members are devout students of the Bible and encourage members and non-members alike to read the scriptures—"a chapter a day." van Dijk (1988:3) asserts that

> the Twelve Tribes accept the Holy Book, from Genesis 1 to Revelation 22, unreservedly and without any restriction. Preference is given to the *Scofield Bible* (1967), but any other version will do as well. That the [W]hite man corrupted the bible when he translated it from the original Amharic, as some Rastas claim, is nonsense according to the Twelve Tribes.

Members believe that only by repeatedly studying the Bible can one receive true wisdom and knowledge of RastafarI. While their attention to the word is strict, they believe that individuals must perceive the Bible according to their own interpretation.

The segments of the Twelve Tribes of Israel are the same as those claimed by individuals who practice the Jewish faith: Reuben, Simeon, Levi, Judah, Dan, Naphtali, Gad, Asher, Issachar, Zebulun, Joseph and Benjamin and Dinah (Genesis 29,30,35). Each name corresponds to a month of the year (beginning with April, Reuben) (see Appendix E) and each is associated with a particular body part, color, and personality trait. These traits correspond to those of the astrological zodiac signs, but Rastas repudiate any connection to this aspect of Babylon.

Women are more numerous among this group than in other Rasta sects and tend to be slightly younger than their male counterparts. Based on one of my fieldwork trips in 1984, I observed that women in this group were more prominent in religious ceremonies than they are in other Rasta groups. According to van Dijk (1988:11) an equal number of women also sit on the executive board. The inclusion of women at this level of organization is unusual, but then, other Rasta groups do not have executive boards. van Dijk states that there is no formal hierarchy on the board, but also notes that "male representatives...are seated in front of the female executives during meetings" (Ibid:11). He also points to an incident of male violence against a woman at a social gathering (Ibid:11).

Williams (1986:23–24) states that women in the Twelve Tribes community that he visited were routinely beaten. This punishment could be meted out for not performing household chores to a man's satisfaction. Williams underscores that Rasta men reject any commentary that such behavior is contrary to notions of "communal bonds." Some Rasta men defend themselves by claiming that criticism regarding violence against women is part of the "White man's strategy to do away with Rasta's fundamental freedom" (Ibid 24). My interviews with Rasta women also revealed that women are subject to male violence, but some women added that it was not as serious (i.e., as frequent) a problem as in the general population.

The Nyabingi

Nyabingi differ from the Twelve Tribes in the sense that they do not consider Haile Selassie a God nor the reincarnation of Jesus Christ, but one among the pantheon of ancestral leaders. The Nyabingi might be characterized as the most left leaning in matters of race consciousness of all of the groups. According to Hopkins (1971:63–65) the term "Nyabingi" derives from an East African group that resisted colonialism until 1928. The term "Nyabingi" signifies "she who possesses many things" and was coined to commemorate a Ruandiaise royal princess who was part of the resistance movement (Ibid:64).

According to the Jamaica Times, (Dec 7, 1935) Haile Selassie was head of the Nyabingi Order whose goal was to overthrow European domination. The racial imperative in this Order struck a familiar chord for Howell who first began to translate the word in terms of violence against people of European descent. "Nyabingi" is also used to refer to a large formal meetings where Rastas of many different persuasions convene.

Among the Nyabingi, the term means "death to the Black and White oppressors" (Reckford 1977:10). In contemporary Jamaica there is hardly a group of Rastas that would be characterized as violent; however, the origin of the term accurately depicts the violent "niyamen" of the 1930s.

The Bobo Shanti

The Ethiopian National Congress, or the Bobo Shanti, are known in Jamaica as the most orthodox Rastas. Like the Nyabingi, they tend to live in groups and adhere to strict religious laws. Their leader, Prince Emmanuel, was one of the early leaders of the movement and was active in organizing Rastas at nyabingis in the 1950s. His strong advocacy for repatriation during this period led to police harassment and ultimately, the destruction of his community in Back-O-Wall.

Claiming divine qualities, as have other Rasta leaders, Emmanuel professes to have materialized on earth in St. Elizabeth in 1915. He fashioned himself as a prototype of Melchizedek, i.e., having neither mother nor father. More recently he has labelled himself god and is considered so by his followers who are primarily located in the hills of St. Thomas in Bull Bay.

The Bobo have very strict rules regarding women's behavior. There are proscriptions regarding women's dress and participation in religious and other arenas. These constraints are based on the belief in women's pollution during menstruation and their alleged inferior status. These beliefs are generally held by all Rastafarians but are applied more strictly within this group. The ideology of pollution is fundamental to the marginalization of women and is discussed more fully in Chapter 6.

The diversity of Rastas notwithstanding, to varying degrees, they all embrace the following general tenets of RastafarI: 1) a belief in the divine power of Haile Selassie; 2) repatriation to Africa; 3) the sacred power of *ganja* (marijuana)[1] ; and 4) women are subordinate to men.

---

1. For more in depth discussion of *ganja* use in Jamaica see Rubin and Comitas (1988) and Chevannes (1988:7–19). For a broader discussion of marijuana consumption and belief systems among Rastafarians see Forsythe (1983) and Barrett (1976:216–218, 128–136).

Selassie I

More recently, one finds many Rastas, but especially those in the upper classes, who assent to Selassie's position as their spiritual leader, but do not consider him a god. Nevertheless, so strong is the general belief in Selassie's divinity that the fact of his death (1975) was repudiated by many Rastas who claim that Selassie has everlasting life. It is a paradox that a group so concerned with the liberation of African people would choose as its leader someone who was anathema to ideals of liberation (Kapuscinski 1983, Mosley 1964).

One could argue that the choice of Haile Selassie as the god of this organization is appropriate given the uneven sexist relations within the movement and the iron fist with which Selassie ruled. One might even suggest that the choice was intentional for these reasons, but it is not clear that Rastafarians, then, as now, were aware of the demagogic rule that Selassie imposed over his kingdom.

During his fifty-odd year reign he improved the infrastructure of Ethiopia by introducing electricity, cars, and a postal service. He also abolished slavery and cruel and unusual punishment, both of which had been integral to Ethiopia for centuries (Kapuscinski 1983:12,15). These improvements notwithstanding, Ethiopia remained a very hierarchical society that was not fundamentally changed and where the vast majority of people were oppressed. In spite of people's abject poverty, Selassie attempted to gain popularity by staging occasional scrap feasts and by showering coins on the multitude. These gestures of largess did nothing to stem mass starvation and widespread illiteracy, but Selassie was more concerned with his own glorification than he was the welfare of his people. He remained a monarch of celebrity status by creating the illusion of virtual divinity by surrounding himself with ministers of ignoble character.

> The King of Kings preferred bad ministers. And the King of Kings preferred them because he liked to appear in a favorable light by contrast. How could he show himself favorably if he were surrounded by good ministers? The people would be disoriented. Where would they look for help (Kapuscinski 1983:33)?

The foremost concern on the mind of a given minister was that of informing the emperor more thoroughly than did the one before him. Using this system, Selassie kept constant discord among them while at the same time receiving complete and accurate information and forcing ministerial loyalty.

For an average Ethiopian citizen, humility obstructed the pathway of justice. In an attempt to make the autocracy look democratic, the monarch allowed the people to submit a list of demands upon the emperor. However, the petitioners were also required by law to kneel face-down when His Imperial Majesty passed by. Some petitions were collected by security personnel, but many were left in the waving hands of those bowed in reverence (Kapuscinski 1983:13). Since illiteracy was widespread, many people sank into years of debt to pay educated persons to write their petitions. The majority of people lived in a state of abject poverty which precluded viable avenues for redress.

By the 1960s the masses of Ethiopians were still not benefitting from Selassie's efforts to "develop" the country. Even though there had been some improvements in education, health, and transportation, ninety percent of the population remained illiterate. Moreover, political power was more centralized than ever, most people were living at a subsistence level with land redistribution essentially nonexistent. The 1973 drought and subsequent famine in the Wello province led to further criticism of the government's corruption and inefficiency. As a consequence of deepening poverty, the absence of land redistribution, and the centralization of power, Selassie's government was overthrown in 1974 by the Dergue (Pankhurst 1992:29; Tareke 1991: 53,57).

In spite of Selassie's malevolent deeds, he became a symbol of freedom and leadership for Rastas. Their unwillingness to critically examine the nature of oppression during his reign is typical of millenarian groups that, by definition, ignore many social and political realities. In the case of Rastafarians, mysticism was carried to an extreme when upon Selassie's death, many Rastafarians believed that he was still alive or that he had simply assumed another form.

A messianic or millenarian religious group is one which focuses on the revitalization of an ideological golden age and one which worships a living or recently deceased person as a god. Haile Selassie fit the bill for Rastafarians since he embodies, at least superficially , all that Rastas stood for. He was an African man, he was a "King of Kings," and a leader of a country that was symbolic of African independence. Even though Rastas' emphasis on African identity is a positive one which has influenced Diaspora Africans everywhere, their ideological transformation of a tyrant into a god, along with their refusal to grapple with the material and political iniquities in society, renders them insulated from other individuals and movements that may be trying to bring about change.

Repatriation to Africa

The second most accepted Rastafarian tenet is the belief in repatriation to Africa as redemptive for African descended people. As mentioned above, while Rastas often cite this principle, for most members, repatriation is more an edifying concept than a reality. While more and more Rastas are actually returning to different parts of Africa (e.g, Ghana, Liberia, and Ethiopia), the vast majority continue to make their homes in Jamaica which they also consider Africa based on their identity as African people.

Many Rastas who have actually repatriated have taken advantage of Haile Selassie's land grant to diaspora Africans and repatriated to Ethiopia.

> At its peak, toward the end of 1970, the settlement of Shashemene [Ethiopia] had between 40–50 Rastas and Afro-Americans, who had set up their community with a pharmacy, a school, a small clinic—named after Dr. Malaku Bayen[2]—a small store and a number of modest dwellings. There were no efforts towards collective farming, hence the problems of individualism, competition and envy plagued the settlers, who eked out an existence (Campbell 1990:224–225).

Shashemene is about 250 kilometers south of Addis Ababa, the capital of Ethiopia (see Figure 2). The Amharic are the predominate cultural group in this agricultural community of about fourteen thousand people. Other groups who inhabit the region include Gurage, Welayita, and Oromo most of whom live in rural areas. Ninety percent of Shashemene inhabitants are Christian and ten percent are Muslim. The Rastafarian community is located north of the center of town on the main road leading from Shashemene.

> [T]he Twelve Tribes of Israel, branches of which exist also in New York City and Jamaica...build their houses with the traditional materials—mud, straw, clay and a loose concrete mixture. The walls of their houses are very porous which, they say, allows them to breathe. These materials will last forever. However, they will not build above the second floor because they know that this would be entering God's realm and defying him. The scriptures prove this with the narrative about the tower of Babel (Lewis 1993:110).

Rastafarian efforts to establish separate communities in Shashemene resulted in reprisals by Ethiopians who were engaged in cooperative farming. Their political position was exacerbated by their devotion to Haile Selassie who was abhorred by most Ethiopians. Even though while in Jamaica more radical Rastas inveigh against capitalism, those in Shashemene have not participated ideologically or actually in the proletarian revolution. Moreover, their anti-European rhetoric is not shared by their neighbors. As a result of the insularity of the Rasta community, they are viewed by many peasants as interlopers. Some Ethiopians usurped Rastafarian land and absconded with their machinery. Fortunately, sympathetic members of the Dergue (as the new Ethiopian regime was called) returned some of the

---

2. Haile Selassie sent Malaku Bayen to New York in 1937 to inaugurate the Ethiopian World Federation.

Figure 2
Ethiopia on the African Continent, with Shashemene

land to them. In spite of these conciliatory efforts on the part of the Ethiopian government, some Rastas left the community.

Jamaican Rastas did not attempt to forge positive relations with Ethiopians. It is ironic that Rastafarians in Jamaica constantly invoke the ideal
of repatriation to Africa, but once there, their beliefs and practices distance them from Ethiopians. According to Lewis (1993) neither are they
accepting of outsiders who do not embrace their way of life. The Ethiopians who Lewis interviewed considered Rastafarian religious and dietary
habits to be very strange. Rastas not only kept to themselves, but when
dealing with Ethiopians in the market, they did not attempt to learn any
of the rules of etiquette regarding casual conversation or greetings. This
and their acerbic attitude created a chasm between them and their long

lost sisters and brothers. A woman who was once married to a Jamaican Rasta

> claimed that newcomers to the commune are soon disillusioned. After staying there and contributing their money to the brethren, they lose heart and leave. The newcomers, she claimed, are exploited and overworked through a process which the brethren call education. If they remain, it is because the brethren put fear in their hearts that the Twelve Tribes in Jamaica will shoot them should they leave. To return to Babylon [the western world] is forbidden and sacrilegious (Ibid 112).

Reportedly, even their relations with Jamaicans who come to visit, or who come with the intention of settling, are alienating. In spite of this, many Twelve Tribes communities around the world send remittances to their flock in Shashemene.

The treatment of women in Shashemene mirrors the subordinate position of women within the organization as a whole. According to a former Ethiopian wife of a Rasta man, women are expected to adhere to strict rules, the transgression of which result in serious physical assaults. She showed Lewis (Ibid 112).

> the scars she bore from such a beating when she was punished for lingering too long in the daily market. Her husband had carefully timed her trips to the market and lateness aroused suspicions of infidelity.

It is my understanding from the literature and anecdotal evidence from people who have visited the community that most of its inhabitants are men who marry Ethiopian women.

In addition to Shashemene, Rastafarian communities have emerged in other parts of Africa and throughout the African Diaspora. Many of these groups in Africa consist of indigenous people who were attracted to Rasta via reggae music (Savishinsky 1994:19–50). Beginning with the reception of calypso in the 1950s, Caribbean music has enjoyed an enthusiastic public in Africa. Reggae has loomed even larger on the African scene mostly as a result of the influence of Bob Marley as a singer and as a cultural icon (Clarke S. 1980; Grass 1984).

Marley's influence has led to a proliferation of Rastafarian groups in various parts of Africa. While scholars of Rasta communities in Africa propose that Rastas attempt to create strong international and pan-African links, these ties have been limited to the adoption of Rastafarian fashion, hair, and cannabis consumption. In fact Savishinsky reports that his informants

> claimed that the spread of reggae and Rastafarianism in West Africa was directly responsible for the upsurge in cannabis use that occurred within the past 10 to 15 years (in Ghana[,] for example, the cultivation and smok-

ing of cannabis has in a relatively brief amount of time, increased to the point where 1990 was officially declared the "year of the War on Wee [weed] [see *People's Daily Graphic,* 6 January 1990]" (1994:29).

In addition to *ganja,* dreadlocks and red, black, green, and gold clothes also mark members of Rasta communities. As in Jamaica, these symbols do not always signify membership into the faith, but an adoption of its superficial aspects. According to Savishinsky "[t]hroughout the region dreadlocks, Rasta colors, and Dread Talk are frequently adopted by young men (Ibid:29)." He goes on to footnote that

> While I did encounter a small number of female Rastas during the course of my research in West Africa, their overall participation in the movement and its attendant forms of cultural expression appeared on the whole to be quite negligible (Ibid:46n12).

It would have been interesting to learn more about even this small number of female Rastafarians in order to help fill the void of research on Rasta women. Clearly more research is needed to determine the degree to which the subordinated position of women in Jamaica is repeated in other parts of the Diaspora and in Africa. It is my guess that women's oppression would be widespread since many of the beliefs about women in Jamaica and the Diaspora as a whole were transported from Africa.

During my own field work in Ghana in 1988 and 1989, while researching Diaspora African repatriates, my visit to the Rasta community in Labadi revealed a preponderance of Ghanaian Rasta men, a few Jamaican men, very few Ghanaian women, and a few European American women. The presence of European and European American "Rastas" is central to the discussion of the historical and cultural significance of Rasta, but one that few scholars have broached.

It is the opinion of many Rastas that anyone who wishes to enter the faith can do so. Others, especially the Nyabingi, adamantly assert that "White" people have no place in RastfarI (White 1984:295). Given the historical genesis of the movement, it is unclear to me how people of European descent can consider themselves as part of RastrafarI, since RastafarI embodies the struggle against European slavery, neo-slavery, and racist oppression. Even though there are some Europeans who pick up the banner of RastafarI, given their white skin advantage, they are unable to escape the benefits of economic and cultural privilege. Moreover, given their privileged position as people of European descent, it is questionable how they can claim the *experience* of African descended people. The willingness of some Rastas to accept European individuals into their fold is yet another indication of their religious versus political foundation.

As for African Rastas as a whole, it appears from the literature that while many Rastas, especially in Anglophone Africa, have embraced some of the religious elements, it is less clear as to whether they have accepted the idea of Selassie as god. Africans in areas that have been directly influenced by Jamaican Rastas, such as Wolde Ab in Ghana and Senegal and Prophet Gad in Ghana, are reportedly more orthodox than other regions (Ibid:32–33). I elaborate on the effects of the diffusion of Rasta and reggae in Chapter Eight.

Rasta Women in England

In addition to Africa, Rastas have migrated to many parts of the globe. Beginning in the early 1950s, many Jamaicans (and other Caribbean populations) saw Britain as an opportunity to increase their chances of finding employment and improving their economic standard.

According to Sheila Patterson (1963:360), the first formal Rastafarian group in England was the United Afro-West Indian Brotherhood established in 1955. The Ethiopian Orthodox Church (EOC) was another organization where Rastas figured prominently. Even though many people consider the EOC to be Rastafarian, it was not in England, nor in Jamaica. In England, the church "forbids its members to wear dreadlocks and, more significantly, refuses to acknowledge the divinity of Haile Selassie" (Ibid:53). In spite of these proscriptions, some Rasta, especially members of the Twelve Tribes, attend EOC services.

Approximately 260,000 Caribbeans emigrated to England in the 1950s and 1960s. Rastafarians were integral to this migrant population. Even though people of African descent were present in England since the sixteenth century, by the end of World War II their numbers grew significantly. These immigrants

> met with disquieting receptions typified most dramatically with the 1958 uprisings in London's Notting Hill and Nottingham's St. Ann's Well Road area when blacks and whites clashed. The emergence of the Teddy Boys as intimidators in the late 1950s was a continual reminder to blacks that they were not valued at least by some sectors of the working class (Cashmore 1979:39).

The passage of the Commonwealth Immigrants Act in 1962 did little to stem the tide of physical violence perpetuated by indigenous Europeans or discrimination in housing and employment. Consequently, Caribbeans withdrew into their own residential enclaves, mostly in London, Birmingham, and Manchester. Given the rejection by Europeans, they also felt compelled to establish their own clubs, stores, and other service institutions. Since the Church of England did not welcome Jamaicans (or other

Caribbean populations) into their congregations, they also established their own churches.

The Pentecostal Church, which was established in 1954, was one of the most vibrant and escapist. Members, who thought of themselves as the chosen people, opted to divorce themselves, as much as possible, from European society and to wait for their reward on Judgement Day. Some of the Pentecostal restrictions included proscriptions against wearing make-up or jewelry, consuming alcohol or tobacco, and sexual promiscuity. Many young people who became Rastas in the 1950s came primarily from Pentecostal families.

The emergence of Rastafarian youth in Britain did not occur in a vacuum. There were several groups such as the Racial Adjustment Action Society (RAAS), the Universal Coloured People's Association (which later became the British Black Panthers), and the Campaign Against Racial Discrimination (CARD) that organized in order to develop political and social solidarity. These groups were heavily influenced by Stokely Carmichael (Kwame Toure) and Malcolm X, both of whom visited England and spoke to audiences on the subject of self-determination. The primary aims of these groups were to establish their own Afrocentric institutions and ideology. Naturally, the British government did not take kindly to what they interpreted as conspiracy against White people and arrested the organizations' leaders. It was within this fluorescence of diaspora African nationalism that RastafarI emerged.

In the 1950's a few Rastafarians were observed in Brixton, but the organization had not yet gained a strong foothold. In the late 1960s Rastafarian themes were mostly regenerated by the Universal Black Improvement Organization (UBIO) which also formed a political wing called the People's Democratic Party. The originators of UBIO, Fox and Gabriel Adams, took advantage of the growing influence of RatafarI, as well as the ideology and symbolism of Marcus Garvey, in order to attract members. UBIO leaders later received permission from the Jamaican Ethiopian World Federation to establish an EWF branch in England. As a consequence of their affiliation with the EWF beginning in the 1970s, Rastas gained more credibility.

As in Jamaica, the majority were members of the lower economic class, with a few middle class people. Cashmore parenthetically mentions the presence and status of Rasta women in Britain during this period.

> Just over one quarter of the membership was comprised of women and their role in Ras Tafari was very much a subordinate one. It was a role graciously accepted by the sisters themselves; new feminism, or women's liberation was regarded as "foolishness, because a woman should do what a man tells her to do" (1979:78).

Given that there are always a range of perspectives within any organization, more in depth research among the women might have uncovered alternative views. Cashmore's *Rastaman* (1979) is an informative work regarding Rastafarians in England, but lends only two pages to Rastafarian women. In his work on "new religions" in England, Peter Clarke (1994:85–88), briefly covers Rastafarian women in four pages. He essentially repudiates the findings by other scholars, mainly Yawney (1983), that male/female dynamics are highly polarized. Clarke concedes that most members believe that women need "to be guided and controlled by the man, the king;" however, he explains this belief away by stating that

> Rasta women...did not feel in any way aggrieved or dissatisfied with their situations (Ibid:87) [and that] women are not in practice confined to the home and often take on the role of breadwinner, going out to work while the man stays home to look after the children (Ibid:88).

Clarke's argument repeats the mistakes made by other scholars in equating women's work outside the home with equality. Moreover, he seems to suggest that because Rastafarian women are not dissatisfied with their lot that sexual dynamics are unproblematic. As one Rastafarian woman in Jamaica noted, "there were also African slaves who did want to be freed."

During my brief visit to London in 1997 I found that there are three major Rastafarian groups: The Twelve Tribes, the Ethiopian World Federation[3], and the Nyabingi. There were also Rastas who were not affiliated with any branch. According to informants there are between 3,000 and 5,000 Rastafarians who live in England and who are mainly concentrated in various parts of London and Birmingham. Most of the women I spoke with lived in South London (in Stockwell, Brixton, and Clapham North). I also spoke with sisters in Birmingham. As is true in Jamaica, there are a range of views among Rasta women in England regarding their status. These differences are partly influenced by individual experience, the particular Rasta group of which they are a part, individual personalities, and the degree of male control in their lives.

Another problem with most analyses of women's status is that there is little ethnographic data to support positions that are taken in the literature. During my visit, I sought to determine the extent of the organization there, "reason" with Rastafarian women, and to ascertain the similarities or differences between Rastafarian women in England and in Jamaica. This was not an in-depth research study, but a preliminary one to fill the paucity of empirical research on Rasta women.

A prevalent Rastafarian belief is that Rasta women must come into the organization through a Rasta man. Many of the women I spoke with chal-

---

3. As mentioned earlier, the Ethiopian World Federation is not by definition Rastafarian. However, in some areas, the links are such that Rastafarians are able to use the EWF title as their own.

lenged this tenet and stated that they became Rasta on their own. However, when asked whether they felt that men were the natural heads of the household, most said that they did. The reasons offered for this belief were mostly economic, supported by Biblical pronouncements. When women suggested that a man should be the head of the family because he is the main economic supporter, this raised the obvious question: "If men are not the primary economic supporters, then, should they still be the head?" One woman then changed her argument and suggested that the man is the head of the household "because he is women's protector." This notion, which is prevalent in many Rasta and non-Rasta societies around the world, never ceases to intrigue me. If it is men who are the main predators of women and these same men who are protecting them, something is amiss. Could it be that it is men who need to be reconditioned to entertain values other than violence against women?

Another woman who was a member of the Twelve Tribes said that the man is "definitely the head of the household." When I again questioned the economic argument, she responded by saying that the man would still be the head since "woman came from man, from Adam's rib. So it is Christ first, then man, then woman." Only a few of the Rasta women I spoke with did not accept the notion that man is the head regardless of his economic position. One woman stated that the "head of [her] household is the Creator."

I also spoke with several Rastafarian men, a few of whom had European and European American female partners. These unions are another factor that has caused dissension among Rastafarians since many men and women object to this practice. Indeed, these mixed unions and their progeny detract from the Afrocentric focus that Rasta initially represented.

Holy Weed

Cannabis sativa is so closely connected with Rastafarians that one might easily think that the frequent use of the herb is peculiar to this group. However, the use of marijuana can be traced back to the ancient history of China, Africa and India where it was used for recreational, religious, and medicinal purposes (Du Toit 1980:11–18; Li 1975). *Ganja*[4] was first brought to Jamaica in 1845 by East Indian indentured servants. The Indian presence not only compensated for the loss of African slave labor, but infused a new religious philosophy and social structure to the island. Along with their subsistence crops, Indians grew *ganja* which caught the interest of their fellow African Jamaican farmers. Indian terminology used to refer

---

4. The first group of Indian indentured servants who migrated to Jamaica between 1845 and 1848 came from the Chota Nagpur area of Bihar, where the use of *ganja* and

to the herb include "Hindi terms such as Khryan (threshing ground), berd (seedling), jharoo (broom), soop (winnowing tray)," (Mansingh and Mansingh 1985:100). These terms, as well as *ganja* itself, are widely used in Jamaica.

The literature also suggests that there are other aspects of RastafarI *ganja* culture that have strong connections with East Indian practices (Hill 1983:35–36). The smoking of the chilum pipe and the reference to *ganja* as Kali are relevant.

Ganja also constitutes one of a myriad of herbs and spices that is a vestige of African pharmacopeia (Campbell 1974; Mitchell 1983:845). Long before the emergence of Rastafarians, Jamaican peasants used *ganja* as an hallucinogen and for culinary purposes. Many Jamaicans can recount stories of their parents soaking *ganja* in white rum and applying it to the skin to treat abrasions or to alleviate painful joints. The herb is also used in cooking and is sometimes added to soup or mixed with milk. My own research among Rastas revealed that *ganja* tea was often administered to infants as a relaxant or to cure a number of ills (Lake 1985:102). It was given to children (in addition to other herbs such as mint, ceresse, and cold bush) in order to treat asthma, colds, fever, or other maladies. In addition to these remedies, *ganja*'s effectiveness in managing glaucoma is well known (West and Lockhart 1978). Clinical trials have also revealed that marijuana is effective in the treatment of diabetes (Robertson 1982:27), inhibiting nausea in terminal cancer (Randall 1990), and in the treatment of AIDS (Grinspoon 1995; Lehrman 1995; Farr 1993), among others.

There are other studies which indicate that the regular use of marijuana is contraindicated. Chronic *ganja* use has been correlated with impotence, infertility, and amotivational syndrome (Winger, Hoffman, and Woods 1992). It is also well known that tetrahydrocannabinol (THC), the psychoactive ingredient in marijuana, readily crosses the placenta and can cause a number of birth defects similar to the ones associated with fetal alcohol syndrome (Braude and Ludford 1984).

With the increased use of *ganja* among Rastafarians, the colonial government enacted the Dangerous Drug Law which came on the heels of International Cannabis legislation in 1931. In spite of these laws, the cultivation and trade continued and *ganja* has been a boon to the Jamaican economy since the 1950s. In the latter part of the twentieth century *ganja* became the leading foreign exchange earner for Jamaica. Despite the centrality of the herb to the Jamaican economy, the government has made stringent efforts to eliminate it.

---

other stimulants was common. *Ganja* was used openly by Indian and African Jamaican farmers until it was banned in 1913 (Mansingh and Mansingh 1985).

Rastafarians claim that *ganja* is divinely inspired and is consumed for "the healing of the Nation." As with many other Rasta practices they purport to receive guidance concerning *ganja* from the holy scriptures.

> And the earth brought forth grass, and herb yielding seed after his kind, and the tree yielding fruit, whose seed was in itself, after his kind: and God saw that it was good (Genesis 1:12).

Other passages used to justify their regular use of the herb include:

> ...thou shalt eat the herb of the field (Genesis 3:18). [and] eat every herb of the land (Exodus 10:12).
> ...He causeth the grass to grow for the cattle, and herb for the service of man....(Psalm 104:14).

The grades and potency of *ganja* (also called wisdom weed, callie and Iley, among others) differ with the particular varieties which are given the following colloquial names:

Alaska	Sensimilla
Skunk	Cambodia
Commercial	Lamb's Bread
Cotton	Thyme
Kali	Tampi

According to my conversations with Rastafarians these terms were originally developed to disguise *ganja* from Babylon. The most potent forms are cotton, skunk, sensimilla, and cambodia.

Ganja consumption is widely practiced among Rasta, but is not universally used. For those who do indulge, many believe that

> ganja is not a chemical drug but an herbal plant divined by Jah [god] for the healing of the [Black] nation as it is a spiritual food or wisdom weed having the power to bring its users to the self-knowledge appropriate and fitting for an awakened and healthy life (Forsythe 1983:119).

One Rasta woman averred that while "many Rastas claim that they smoke herb to receive divine inspiration, in fact, they use it in the same way other people do—merely to get high." While it is difficult to prove that Rastas do not smoke *ganja* for religious purposes, it is also unclear what they have been divinely inspired to do.[5]

One of mythologies circulating about Rasta women is that they do not smoke *ganja*. Although it is more common to see Rasta (and other) men smoking *ganja* in public, all but one of the Rasta women that I have spoken with smoked the herb. Rastafarian mothers also administered *ganja* tea to their children more often than other informants with whom I spoke.

---

5. See Taylor (1984) regarding legal issues around the sacramental use of marijuana.

In spite of this widespread use, Rastafarians' affinity to marijuana consumption is one of the main reasons why other Jamaicans view them disparagingly.

While colonial officials encouraged the use of *ganja* among nineteenth century indentured servants, and turned a blind eye to its use in the early part of the twentieth century, in the 1970s Jamaican officials cooperated with the United States government in devising a plan to systematically eradicate *ganja* fields. This task was initiated under the rubric of Operation Buccaneer which included the spraying of fields with glyphosphate, a chemical which, reportedly, has no toxic effects on the soil and has a low toxicity to humans. In spite of these efforts, *ganja* has continued to proliferate in Jamaica (Daily Gleaner 1993:1). The literature suggests that its cultivation, consumption, and export continue because of the high level of corruption among police and government officials (Stone 1991; Lacey 1977).

Chapter 5

The Interface between Sexism and Capitalism

Women in Jamaica and the rest of the African diaspora are subordinated to men politically, economically, culturally, and physically (Sen and Grown 1987; Safa 1986; Lindsay 1980). As shown in Figure 3 (see p. 80), their marginalization in any one sphere does not stand alone, but exists in tandem with all other forms of containment. This chapter outlines the symbiotic relationship between economics and government and how these institutions systematically oppress women. A cultural ethos that emanates from kinship and religious institutions, and that is reified in schools and in media, provide the superstructural components of women's marginalization.

I suggest that women's distance from the means of production and their inferior economic position relative to men set the stage for their marginalization in other areas. This structural containment creates an environment where men abuse their sexual mobility, attempt to contain that of women, and, with impunity, subject women to physical violence (Jones, A. 1987). In every phase of Jamaican history, women's economic and political marginalization has preceded other forms of containment.

Political Marginalization

Government and politics have always been gatekeepers for economic structures, and in Jamaica, as elsewhere, these institutions have kept women at the recesses of socio-economic prosperity. In fact, there is little difference between the dynamics of capitalist enterprises and the government. The latter creates the legal environment (such as "free trade" agreements between Third World and First World nations) for the exploitation of labor and allows big business to more easily convert raw materials into commodities for sale on the international market (McAfee 1991:82–91). Women have encompassed the largest proportion of laborers who have provided the fuel for new international labor agreements and serve as pawns in a system of government within which they have no control.

Although women constitute a slight majority in the Jamaican population, they have never held positions of political leadership or power. This is typical of the Caribbean at large where only two women, Eugenia Charles

Figure 3

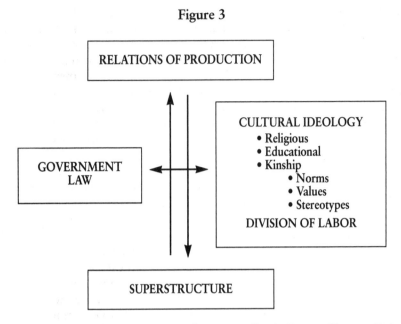

(Prime Minister of Dominica) and Maria Liberia-Peters (former Prime Minister of the Netherlands Antilles), have held major political offices. Even the presence of women Prime Ministers does not necessarily change the status or opportunities of women or poor people in general since women in positions of influence have had a tendency to support the national and international power relations thereby maintaining the status quo. For example, Eugenia Charles' decision to support U.S. hegemony by sending troops into Grenada to extinguish the leadership of Maurice Bishop is the most glaring illustration of how women in powerful positions have worked to support imperialist forces.

More recently, Portia Simpson, Jamaica's Minister of Labor under Patterson's regime, tried to convince Jamaicans that the process of growth has "not been without difficult moments but overall we have done very well" (Simpson 1997:B5). A cursory look at the conditions of poverty in Jamaica would belie this claim of doing "very well." Articles by other Jamaican citizens abound in the daily tabloids regarding the deepening poverty and other indignities that Jamaicans are forced to endure (see, e.g., Espeut 1997:A4; Walters 1997:7). Given that the few women who have taken leadership roles are chosen because of their willingness to tow the party line, clearly it is not just female leadership that is important, but leadership by women and men who are invested in real change and in the self-determination of African descended people.

Presently, women have been active in local level politics. Although they constitute a major force as campaign workers and organizers, their influence "is largely confined to the lowest levels of political party structure and the inclusive State apparatus; they are not highly visible in the decision-making echelons" (Harrison 1988:116). At the local level women are dominated by male party leaders or brokers and are often coerced into becoming "friendly" with these men in order to gain political favors (Ibid:16). Even though historically women have not held political power, many feminist and anthropology scholars have attempted to create women's power where it does not exist.

There is an abundance of general anthropological literature that attempts to locate women's power in various informal social settings (Rodriguez J.1994; Leacock 1981; Sudarkasa 1987). This discourse ignores the significance of control over the means of production and the ramifications of this control in other spheres. Many scholars have limited women's "power" to a minority of women holding leadership positions among women, women's increasing numbers in the work force, and even gossip networks. These assertions are absurd and obfuscate male dominance over the masses of women. When power is defined as control over cultural and material resources, the oppression of women is clear. That women in Jamaica are denied equal access to material resources is well known (Senior 1991; Spaulding 1993; Antrobus and Gordon 1984; Antrobus 1987; Davies and Anderson 1987).

To say that women are oppressed is not tantamount to saying that they have no influence or agency at all and that they can be manipulated at men's will. It does mean that men hold the most powerful portions in political and economic spheres, which, in turn means that, given men's penchant to abuse power, capitalism will remain the political economic system that superexploits women above and beyond other working class people.

Economic Marginalization

Women in Jamaica have always been at the bottom of the economic hierarchy, a position which encourages their dependence on and abuse from men. The economic condition of female African Jamaicans after slavery is delineated in Chapter 2. The data on women at the turn of the century is not very abundant or revealing (Lobdell 1988; Brodber 1986). We do know that late nineteenth and early twentieth century male migration to Cuba and Panama influenced labor conditions and that,

the rate of growth of working age men was less than the rate of growth of working age women in rural parishes in the intercensal periods up to

1921. But during the years 1921–1943, all parishes experienced higher growth rates of working age men as compared with working age women (Lobdell 1988:208).

From 1891 to 1921 men dominated the professional occupations and women were found in higher proportions in agriculture and domestic spheres. Lobdell (1988:216) reports that this was probably due to growth in the agricultural sector and a reduction in the male working age population.

As noted above, the effects of the 1938 Rebellion, while considered by some to be a watershed event for certain sectors of the populace, was retrograde for women since European men in government positions as well as African and mulatto men further galvanized the culture of domesticity. The laws set in place by the Moyne Commission and the cultural ethos that normalized women's dependency are indicative of the superstructural institutions in law and family that sustain and support women's economic status.

The recession periods in the 1970s had a negative impact on all working class people, but given the history of women's marginzalization, women were doubly affected. IMF austerity policies reduced wages and accelerated capital intensive development. These policies resulted in a reduction in human services and rising unemployment hitting women the hardest. During the 1970s the average rate of unemployment was 39% for women and 16% for men. In the 1980s unemployment rates increased for both women and men, with women continuing to be more often unemployed than men. Table 3 shows that even though unemployment decreased over time, the rates were high in general and the gap between women and men was consistent.

In 1996, 23 percent of women were unemployed compared to 10 per cent of men, which represented a slight increase for women compared to 1995 figures (*The Labour Force* 1996:33). The overall unemployment rate was 16 percent.

Moreover, employed women experience discrimination in the workplace and receive lower pay in traditionally female occupations. "Even where women have similar qualifications, perform similar tasks and have the same level of productivity, their remuneration is usually significantly lower than their male counterparts" (Levitt 1991:48). Among the forty percent of Jamaican women who are heads of households (i.e., they do not have permanent live-in male partners) many are economically dependent on men who enjoy temporary or visiting relationships.

In addition to the feminization of poverty in urban areas, women who work on small holder agricultural systems in rural areas are also at a disadvantage. In part, this disadvantage results from the division of labor where women usually produce crops for local consumption and men produce cash crops. An analysis of LeFranc's study indicates that higglers fare better than full-time small farmers, but this is more a commentary on the

Table 3
Unemployment Rates by Sex, 1972–1990
(Percentages)

Year	Male	Female	Both Sexes
1972	14.5	33.4	22.9
1973	13.4	33.8	22.5
1974	12.7	30.6	20.7
1975	11.9	31.7	20.9
1976	14.7	35.6	24.2
1977	14.6	34.6	23.8
1978	15.7	37.7	26.0
1979	19.9	43.5	31.0
1980	16.0	38.9	26.8
1981	14.2	38.9	25.6
1982	17.0	40.5	27.9
1983	16.2	38.4	26.7
1984	15.7	36.5	25.4
1985	16.1	36.6	25.6
1986	13.3	32.6	22.3
1987	13.6	29.5	20.8
1988	11.9	27.0	18.9
1989	9.5	25.2	16.8
1990	9.3	23.1	15.7

Statistical Institute of Jamaica, (See Panton 1993:116).

low remuneration gained from farming than it does the welfare of higglers (1996:110).

Moreover, the migration of male household members to jobs off the farm makes women's work even more burdensome. Women are left to perform child care and household duties single handedly. Often these responsibilities become too onerous and women join the ranks of rural-urban migrants (Chaney and Lewis 1985). However, recent studies have shown that it is primarily women with secondary and tertiary educations who are migrating to urban areas.

Many women are self-employed and earn money by participating in small-scale, labor intensive activities. This informal sector[1], which encom-

---

1. This is a widely used term to describe self-employment in many Third World countries. I find the term troublesome since it suggests that economic endeavors where people are, to a large extent, earning income based on their own agency and initiative is less legitimate than those within the bureaucracy. I use the term self-employed whenever possible, but when addressing the literature which refers to different categories within the "informal sector" I use the author's terms. At the same time, I suggest that as scholars with the

passes one third to one half of the work force in Jamaica (Anderson 1987), consists of three sectors: the urban informal, the rural farm informal, and the rural non-farm informal. The rural farm informal sector constitutes the largest sector (58%) which is composed of farmers engaged in small scale production. The remainder of the self-employed work force is made up of higglers who are mainly concentrated in urban areas (Panton 1993:87).[2] Higglers sell a number of items either produced by themselves or by others which include food, household items, and *ganja*, to name a few.[3] While some higglers who work in rural areas are faring better than some teachers, clerical workers, and unskilled labour, this is not to say that higglers, in general, are well off, but that the wage scale in these other sectors is very low.

Higgling, by definition, allows women to earn very little pay, offers no insurance, and is unstable by nature. LeFranc (1996:110) notes that most higglers in urban areas are "at the bottom of the economic hierarchy." On average, the majority of higglers do not make over J$1,000 (approximately US$182) per week. This means that the majority of higglers are making less than US$9,000 per year with some urban higglers making as little as US$428 annually. LeFranc's research is significant since it dispels the myth of the higgler as a powerful woman, an exemplar of the Jamaican "matriarch."

Jamaican women (as well as women of African descent in all parts of the diaspora) are often described as matriarchal—strong, independent, and powerful. This mystification of Jamaican women, especially poor women, does them more harm than good since it confuses the obligation of working independently in order to survive with power. Women are often forced into low paying, arduous, and unstable occupations because they have no other options. Often with children in tow, higglers work their way to the market or to the city streets to sell their wares in competition with a number of other women selling similar items. Douglass (1992) clearly delineates the inherent contradiction regarding the mystification of the higgler's status.

> To say that Jamaica is a matriarchy or that women such as the higgler
> rule over men in Jamaica is less a claim than a joke. The higgler is viewed
> as a comical character, a caricature of a woman, whose reputed strength
> of character contrasts to her lack of power. Indeed, although she is high-

---

authority to define others, we search for a term that lends more dignity to people's own efforts.

2. Higglers are formally known as Informal Commercial Traders.

3. For an in-depth discussion of Jamaican higglers, see Elsie LeFranc (1996) and Patricia Anderson (1987).

ly independent and self-sufficient, women like the higgler possess little of
Jamaica's economic and political power (Douglass 1992:248).

Higglers are part of a continuum of working women in Jamaica who
are increasingly dependent on foreign capital. The International Monetary Fund's imposition of Structural Adjustment Programs (SAPs) differ-
entially impact on women's welfare. In Jamaica, as in the rest of the Third
World, Export Processing Zones, which are integral to SAP operations,
exploit women as a cheap labor source which fuels the coffers of local
and international capitalists (Deere et al. 1990; Antrobus 1987; Bolles
1996; Davies and Anderson 1987). SAPs continue to increase the level of
unemployment and lower wages for women while the cost of goods and
services steadily increases. These programs were organized as part of the
Caribbean Basin Initiative (CBI) by Ronald Reagan and subsequently by
George Bush. Bush's 1990s design, the Enterprise for the Americas Initiative, intensified CBI operations and facilitated the transfer of U.S. companies to the island.

In 1991, the United States invested U.S. $770 million into the Jamaican
economy most of which was channeled into the booming garment industry. While international capitalists pretend that the purpose of such investments is to reduce the Jamaican national debt and to increase employment, an opposite scenario persists. Foreign initiatives, whether they are
called Caribbean Basin Initiative, Enterprise for the Americas, or Export
Processing Zones, all spell unemployment and deepening poverty for the
masses of people. As indicated in Table 1, unemployment rates for women
have not significantly improved since the late 1980s and far outstrip those
of men. Even the employed sectors are negatively affected by the imposition of foreign control.

> In 1991, on the recommendation of the IMF, the government abolished sub-
> sidies of basic foods, both domestic and imported. The IMF agreement
> also allowed devaluation of the Jamaican dollar, thereby cheapening
> exports and rendering imports more expensive (Bolles 1996:114).

In addition to the decline in availability of food, poor people in Jamaica
have been adversely affected by a general deterioration in basic services
such as health care, education, nutrition, and shelter. Austerity measures
brought about by IMF policies would be devastating in any event, but are
especially so in Jamaica where the cost of living is considerably higher than
in the United States.

Under such conditions, the majority of Jamaicans are struggling to survive.
The relative lack of opportunities for women in the job market and their
added child care and household responsibilities exacerbate the feminization
of poverty.

Culture as Ideology

At the level of culture, or ideology, ideas about the subordination of women are pervasive. Kinship, education, media, and religious institutions provide arenas where women are deemed inferior and where their subordinate positions are sacralized. The role of religion in the derogation of women is central to our discussion since religion is a fundamental and largely unchallenged aspect of people's culture. This is unfortunate since it is the ostensible sacredness of religious thought that makes it so dangerous. Religious ideology is no more than human thought which is written in Biblical form so as to create a mystique of righteousness around everyday behaviors.

Christianity is one of the primary sources that edifies the cultural ethos of violence and abuse that dehumanizes women. In the Christian Bible, as in other religious texts, women are idolized and at the same time represented as the embodiment of sin. Throughout the Bible, this latter characterization serves as a charter for all forms of violence against females (Brown 1994:1–10). Slave women, concubines, virgins, daughters—all manner of females are given to men to do with as they will. Levite's concubine (who is unnamed) is gang raped by a mob of men (Judges 1); women are taken as prisoners of war (Genesis 34:29; Numbers 31:18); and men who sexually violate women are not condemned. Instead, they are obliged to pay restitution (bride price) to her father (Genesis 22:16f)—a practice which forms stronger bonds among the men across family lines and one which moves women around like pawns. These examples are abundant and point to the institutionalization of violence against women and the lack of control women have over their own bodies.

Although many students of the Bible are quick to point out that there are Biblical passages that honor women's capabilities, in a fundamental sense, women are depicted as naturally subordinate to men. Ways in which sacred texts and rituals are manipulated to ensure the subordinate status of women is delineated in Chapter 6. Religious texts are joined by other institutions that reinforce and legitimate men's superior position.

Representation of Women in Media

Media significantly contribute to the creation of stereotypical norms that perpetuate the idea of women as subservient beings with nothing to offer other than their sex and domestic services. In general, women are represented as docile, passive, and less intelligent than men. Television programming, both local and imported varieties, reify women's roles as housekeepers and vehicles for men's sexual pleasure. In the print media as well, women are almost always represented as sexual objects with no other interests except providing pleasure to men and maintaining their households.

In 1993 a study of women in Caribbean media was organized through the Caribbean Institute of Mass Communication (CARIMAC), UWI (Mona). This study reports that women are found at the lower echelons and work as reporters, presenters, and editors. Very few work in middle or top management or policy making positions (National Report on the Status of Women [NRSWJ] 1995:86). The study went on to report that although women are present on the Board of Directors, they do not constitute more than 20 to 30 percent. In addition, the stereotyping of women is evidenced by their relative absence as engineers, camera operators, and sports reporters (Ibid 87). CARIMAC is joined by a number of other groups who are concerned about the negative images of women in print and electronic media. In response to these representations, Sistren has established a Women's Media Watch which monitors media messages for representations that demean and promote violence against women (National Report on the Status of Women 1995:88).

This work is significant because negative representations of women are a reflection of those operating in the household and other spheres so that they serve to reinforce normative behavior. Because these images are so pervasive, they are internalized by both men and women as natural attributes of women, thus validating the idea of male superiority. This is not only true for Jamaican women, but for women around the world.

Kinship and Education

In Jamaica, the lines between what it means to be female versus male are very distinct. At a very young age girls are expected to carry out domestic chores. At puberty girls are more limited in their mobility than boys and are more often restricted to the yard. If they venture from home, it is usually for the purpose of performing some domestic related chore, where "boys are free to engage in non-purposive activities outside of the confines of the yard" (Chevannes 1985:8). These roles are internalized since parents are known to exact severe sanctions if children act out of their prescribed roles.

According to Chevannes (1985:8) after age five, parents emphasize modesty and proper sexual behavior to their female children. Since boys are given more freedom than girls, and men who are permanent or visiting members of the household have privileges over women, girls are conditioned from an early age to accept men as the heads of households regardless of their economic contribution (Powell 1986). Thus kinship institutions are places where children are socialized by gendered prescriptions that heavily influence their behaviors.

In a 1985 national study of eight hundred randomly selected men (Chevannes 1985), most informants indicated that they were positively disposed to participating in domestic chores usually preserved for women; however, in practice, they did not regularly participate in these activities. Most of the men in this study also considered themselves to be the heads of the family. Other studies (Powell 1986; Douglass 1992) have found that women, in spite of their responsibility for most household matters, defer to men as the heads of households.

Lisa Douglass (1992) cogently argues that Jamaican women are subordinate to men regardless of their class or status. Even when men are not permanent members of the household, women defer to their visiting male partners and male relatives.

> On the occasions when a man...chooses to come home, the woman gives priority to his needs. She prepares his favorite food, turns on the television for him, and silences the children so that, for the limited time he chooses to stay, the man enjoys the privileges of being the head of household (Brodber 1975:43–44).

The same holds for upper class women who defer to men more regularly given that they are more often married and their status is closely connected to the status of their husbands. This is significant since part of what defines masculinity is a man's ability to "receive the services and request the attention of women" (Douglass 1992:251). Advantages and increased opportunities in the home are reinforced in educational institutions.

Engendering Girls and Boys

The prima facie evidence regarding girls' educational performance would suggest that women would have more opportunities in society and higher remuneration than men. Even though more girls attend school than boys and perform better on standardized tests, we do not see this reflected in their economic status after graduation. Moreover, even though girls are participating more regularly in medicine and other sciences, they continue to be segregated in other fields.

According to Elsa Leo-Rhynie (1987:20–21) "the Caribbean Examination Council (CXC) of 1984 and 1985...reveals [that] (g)ender biases in specific subject areas are...evident. Girls predominate in the study of the traditionally female areas:

Clothing and Textiles:	5 boys	761 girls
Shorthand:	6 boys	873 girls
Home Management:	9 boys	952 girls
Woodwork:	831 boys	24 girls

Metalwork: 624 boys   8 girls
General Electricity   722 boys   50 girls"

Sex segregation continues at the tertiary level at the University of the West Indies (in Jamaica, Barbados and Trinidad) where there is

> a concentration of women in Arts and General Studies (approximately 3 women to 1 man)[,] in Education (2 women to each man), and in Nursing, where all thirteen (13) persons registered were women. There was a slightly higher female registration in Law and Social Sciences (Ibid:22).

Other studies (Bailey 1987) corroborate these findings and point to ways in which educational programs reify stereotypes. In the Human Employment and Resource Training (HEART) programme there is

> a concentration of men in Engineering (8 men to each woman), in Medical Sciences (2 men to 1 woman), and a slightly higher male registration in Natural Sciences and Agriculture (Leo-Rhynie 1987:23).

What is significant about these disparities is that they translate into occupational differences where men invariably receive higher wages than women. Moreover, while there is a higher number of girls who complete high school and go on to tertiary education (Gordon, D. 1996), there remains a high percentage of girls who drop out of school due to pregnancy. Studies have indicated that this often occurs due to a lack of knowledge about human biology and contraception. MacCormack (1985) sampled 268 women at an anti-natal clinic and found that a lack of information about human anatomy, combined with folk beliefs, contributed to the non-utilization of contraceptives. Other studies that focus on the relationship between education and fertility corroborate these findings (Whittaker 1980; Justus, McKenzie, and Powell 1979).

Justus et al. (1979) indicated that there was a negative correlation between fertility and educational achievement. Comparing student achievement at High Schools and New Secondary Schools, Justus found that the number of students who dropped out due to pregnancy was almost twice as high at the New Secondary Schools than in the High schools. That the latter institutions reportedly offer a better quality education cannot be overlooked. Economic class plays an important part in this process, since families who are economically better off are more able to send their children to higher quality schools.

Male Violence Against Women

In addition to their economic and social marginalization, women are routinely subject to male violence. This violence is sometimes inflicted by

Table 4
Number of Reported Rape Cases*

1988	1016
1989	1032
1990	1006
1991	1091
1992	1108

*Cases reported to police. (NRSWJ 1995:69)

Table 5
Rape Cases Reported and Adjudicated, 1994–1995

1994		1995	
Reported	Cleared Up	Reported	Cleared Up
1251	636	1605	563

strangers, but is more often carried out by husbands and other male partners, male relatives, or other men who are known to the victims. Rape, one of the more devastating forms of violence against women, has been on the increase since 1961 when 142 cases were reported. By 1973, 641 cases were reported and only 296 offenders were sentenced. The data listed in Table 4 show an increase in the number of cases reported beginning in 1988.

Even with this sharp increase in numbers, they are probably underestimates since many females do not report rape cases for fear of retribution, disbelief, or harassment by authorities. Efforts on the part of the authorities to apprehend the perpetrators of these crimes are indicated in Table 5.

In Jamaica, as in the U.S. and other parts of the Diaspora, the excuse often given for rape is that it is "a product of a man's sense of powerlessness within the system" (Gordon, L. 1986:80). This is a weak response at best. At worst, it adds to the myriad of societal factors that perpetuate male power over women. Rape, as with other forms of physical violence, is no less than men exercising their sexual and physical power over women in a world where male dominance is an acceptable norm. Rape often goes unpunished because it is men who predominate in enforcement and judicial institutions and who operate to protect the status quo (Phillips 1988:38–57).

Although members of the criminal justice system state that it is difficult to apprehend rapists because women often fail to press charges, victims are often dissuaded from doing so. In a case where a 32-year old business executive was gang raped by six men, she reported that

[a]bsolutely nothing happened, although I was able to give [the police] some leads to help find the suspected offenders. Many months after the incident, I was invited to an identification parade and when I walked into the police station I got the feeling that I was in the enemy camp. I panicked and ran. I wanted to do the right thing but I did not get the feeling of being supported (Gordon, L. 1986:81).

In addition to rape by strangers, rape and other forms of violence by male partners is common. The fact that husbands have the legal right to rape or otherwise sexually abuse their wives is a clear indication that the government is not moving in a direction that will give women more power over their bodies (French and Bonner 1989).

Some women feel compelled to withstand this violence in order to maintain the (often meager) financial help they receive from men. Others have been conditioned to accept it as a way of life. Even though women's organizations are active in educating women about their legal rights regarding domestic violence, women often feel stuck in undesirable domestic situations due to the burdens that often come with high parity and having children very early in life.

In spite of laws which inveigh against domestic and other forms of violence against women and girls, these laws are superseded by a cultural ethos that treats females as second class citizens. Moreover, many women have been so conditioned to consider themselves incomplete without men that they feel it necessary to tolerate them at any cost. For women who do seek to terminate their marital bonds, the new divorce laws make it more difficult for them to extricate themselves from an undesirable situation since the law works to reconcile couples even when both parties see the relationship as irretrievable (NRSWJ 1995:29).

There are several women's groups that have formed in the past decade to address these issues. For example, WOMAN, Inc. established a Women's Crisis Center in 1985. This organization provides training skills for women from eighteen to twenty-five years old in an effort to provide them with the human capital that would reduce their dependence on men. The Crisis Center also records statistics on all forms of violence against women and provides support to women who are victims or rape and other kinds of sexual abuse. This and other forms of shelter address the immediate needs of female victims and are much needed short term measures that will help women in times of emergency. However, male violence will continue to be a serious problem until men in the criminal justice system become as outraged by these egregious acts as women. Moreover, women need to see themselves as independent actors and form women's organizations that allow them to protect themselves, by any means necessary.

Incest

Incest is another form of male violence where girls are raped or otherwise sexually abused by relatives. Dr. D. Eldemire of the University of the West Indies asserts that it is difficult to obtain statistics on the number of cases due to the problem of non-reporting. Much of the data that is available is uncovered by the incidence of sexually transmitted diseases in young children and by reports made to the Department of Social and Preventative Medicine (Ross-Frankson and Fletcher n.d.:20). Dr. Eldemire reports that at one clinic, in

> 12 of 16 cases of substantiated rape, the man alleged to be responsible was known to the child although sometimes the actual name was not known. In 14 of 16 cases, the sexual act took place in or around the home of the child. Four of the children were given money (Ibid:20).

In this same study Eldemire found that in nine out of seventeen cases the male was the only parent in the household. Four out of the seventeen children stated that their fathers would beat them if they refused their sexual advances.

Children who are victims of incest and who are members of two parent households often received no help from their mothers who also feel threatened by the perpetrator. Thus some mothers elect to hush up the incidents rather than report them to the police. Often when children divulge the abuse to their mothers, they are "blamed, boxed or beaten" (Ibid:21). The children in Eldemire's study ranged from two to sixteen years old.

Rastafarian women are not set apart from other Jamaican women in the area of domestic violence and sexual assault. According to Rasta women whom I interviewed, their experiences are different only in degree and not in kind. In the following chapter I elaborate on the influence of cultural and religious ideologies that subordinate Rastafarian women and, by association, other Jamaican women.

Chapter 6

The Sacralization of Sexism

In most societies, religious ideology is created and promulgated by men and characterizes women as close to sin and men as close to God (Uta 1990; Raming 1976; Beers 1992; Dunfee 1989; Goldenberg 1979). While most people consider religious texts to be sacred, in actuality, they are only sacred because human culture has made them so. Religious texts are no more than a set of rules laid down by men which reflect or support the existing moral order.

In Christianity, Islam, Judaism, and other religions, women are deemed polluted or sinful because they are women. In this chapter I argue that Rastafarian women are doubly oppressed compared to other Jamaican women since they are subject to proscriptions inherent in Christian doctrines and practices inherent to traditional African cultures. Before elaborating on these issues, it is important to recognize the misogynist tendencies of other religious doctrines.

Under Jewish law, "(m)en and women are expected to follow different routes in the pursuit of the ideal life that God has prescribed for them" (Webber 1983:143). Women are denied certain religious duties, are segregated in the synagogue, and are considered impure during menstruation and childbirth (Renzetti and Curran 1989:268–272; Hyman 1976; Ruether 1974). The degree of these proscriptions depends upon the level of orthodoxy, but at all levels women are not given equal status or opportunities.

Islam is equally clear on where women belong in relationship to men. Although the Qur'an emphasizes justice and equality for all human beings, it also proposes that men are the "guardians" of women and "a degree above" them (Ahmed 1992:678–679). While the Muslim scriptures set the stage for the unequal status of men and women, interpretation of these texts justifies political and cultural containment of women (Renzetti and Curran 1989:276–277).

In India Hindu women are compared to the goddess, *pativrata*, who represents the idyllic woman, one who exhibits chastity, purity, and absolute loyalty to her husband. Women's behavior is modelled on this mythology and women are sanctioned if they fail to emulate this ideal. Throughout much of the history of India, many Hindu women were led to believe that it was their duty to commit ritual suicide on their husbands' funeral pyres in order to demonstrate their devotion to them (Narasimhan 1990). More accurately, widow immolation is symbolic of men's ownership of their wives. Since widows were viewed as pariahs by many people in India, they often felt obliged to commit ritual suicide given their isolation. The examples of ways in which religion serves as a fifth column in women's oppression are never ending.

Nevertheless, religion is rarely criticized for its derogation of women since most people perceive religious writing as sacred and, therefore, above scrutiny. This reluctance to address religious discourse as an ideology is antiprogressive since religious hierarchy is inconsistent with women's opportunities for equality. Religious texts are just that—texts. They were written by human hands, and like other texts, they contain the ideas and prejudices prevalent in society at large. Christian doctrine was written by men who, in their everyday lives, considered women to be servants for their needs and vessels for their sexual pleasure. Moreover, these texts symbolically usurp women's biological capacity to bring forth human life.

This reasoning is most clearly reflected in the concept of the Virgin Mary. If Mary is pure based on her virginity, then it follows that all other non-virgin women must be tainted. Not only are women vilified based on their powers of natural procreation, but the notion that a male god has made this virgin birth possible symbolically usurps from women the power of giving birth.

> All mainstream religious traditions...replace the wonder of women's reproductive power with stories of creation by a male god. In one of the two creation myths in Genesis, god created Eve out of Adam's rib to be his partner (rather than a being with her own purposes) [Genesis-2:18–23, New English Bible]. Eve tempts Adam and her reproductive power becomes a punishment for sin in the story of the fall [Genesis 3:16–19, New English Bible]. Because of her sin, God declared Adam her master. Christianity adds, as a prerequisite of true life, rebirth through redemption by a male god (Becker 1994:4–5).

So what males cannot accomplish in real life, they capture in literature created only by themselves. Having established the "natural" vilification of the female, the Bible goes on to relegate women to an impure status.

Pollution as Cultural Ideology

The idea that women are polluted, which is embodied in Christian dogma and African traditional beliefs, constitutes the theoretical basis for the subordination of Rastafarian women. In addition to women's normal discharges during sex, her capacity to give birth and to menstruate is also considered a sin. The claim that women are polluted is significant because it lays the groundwork for her elimination from full participation in social, political, and economic spheres.

> [Pollution] is used in the context of sex and gender and refers to the capacity that women have to endanger men through their bodily substances and through their overall femaleness (Faithorn 1975:130).

The idea of female pollution is ubiquitous among human societies (Ullrich 1992; Meigs 1991; Buckley and Gottlieb 1988) and is predicated on biblical teaching.

> A woman who becomes pregnant and gives birth to a son will be ceremonially unclean for seven days, just as she is unclean during her monthly period. On the eighth day the boy is to be circumcised. Then the woman must wait thirty-three days to be purified from her bleeding....If she gives birth to a daughter, for two weeks the woman will be unclean, as during her period. Then she must wait *sixty-six* (emphasis added) days to be purified from her bleeding (Leviticus 4:12).

Although men's discharges are also considered unclean (Leviticus 4:15), their days of atonement are much less than those of a woman. The longer period of purification required of women who have female children is indicative of their alleged inferior status.

Men in Judeo-Christian tradition also exhibit their power through violence (see, for example, Psalm 7:12–13). Women, on the other hand, are, by and large, represented as passive beings who are expected to submit to their husbands' rule, mostly because women have been cursed by God. In Genesis, upon discovering that Adam and Eve have eaten the forbidden fruit, God states,

> I will greatly increase your pangs in childbearing;
> In pain you shall bring forth children,
> Yet your desire shall be for your husband,
> And he shall rule over you (Genesis 3:16).

The longevity of Christian dogma among Africans in Jamaica render Jamaican women susceptible to the idea that women are of lesser value than men. These messages are powerful enough in and of themselves; however, combined with derogatory stereotypes and characterizations on television, movies, and secular texts, they become normalized and internalized as natural codes of behavior.

The acceptance of Christian tenets is not limited to Rastafarian women; however, the interpretation and activation of these rules is more tightly adhered to by Rasta than by other Jamaican women. While all Rastafarian women do not consider themselves subordinate to Rasta men, many do. These feelings of inferiority are, in part, the result of a religious ideology that depicts women as polluted.

Rastafarian women are considered polluted during menstruation. During this period they must remain isolated from "free" (nonmenstruating) women and from men. When Bobo Shanti women are menstruating, they must go into seclusion where they do not touch any food, clothing, or other belongings of men or "free" women. Given their alleged defiled status, they are also prohibited from attending any social or religious events. I should hasten to say that even though these practices are widely held, they are more prevalent among women who live in Rasta communities.

During an interview session with Rasta women in Bull Bay, I asked the group if a Rastafarian woman could be a minister in the church. Although I had expressly arranged to speak with Rasta women, a man came into the room and imposed himself onto the conversation and made the following proclamation.

> A woman can't speak to the congregation. You can't have women preachers going up on a pulpit...her nakedness could be displayed. The man creates everything so he must be the head. That's why the world is like it is because women are doing too many things that she shouldn't be doing. It is an abomination for woman to do things pertaining to man and vice versa.

This quote clearly reveals this man's sense of his omnipotence even to the point of being the *creator* of all things. That he absorbed the Christian teaching that defines women's position in the church is indicated by his near replication of Corinthians XIV:34–35.

> Let your women keep silent in the churches, for they are not permitted to speak; but they are to be submissive. If they want to learn something, let them ask their own husbands at home, for it is shameful for women to speak in the church.

This passage is remarkable for at least two reasons. It assumes that all women will be married and that their inferiority (also assumed) should render them voiceless. This position is redolent of African puberty rites that admonish girls to speak in a soft voice (Brain 1978:180).

In many Rastafarian communities, women are forbidden from being preachers because of their alleged polluted status. This subservient position is prevalent in Jamaica at large.

> Though religion and sex interface across a broad frontier, one particularly interesting link is that which sees the role of preaching as an essentially male sexual activity and the role of church attendance and worship as an essentially female sexual activity (Chevannes 1995:33).

Similar to female/male relations in the United States, congregations are mainly made up of women who also do most of the fund raising, social work, and cooking while men assume formally recognized positions of leadership. Even though African American women are not formally considered polluted, their relegation to second class status is similar to that experienced by women in Jamaican society.

The ostensible uncleanliness of Rasta women lays the groundwork for her submissiveness. Although all Rastafarian women are aware of beliefs about the impurity of women during menstruation, the Bobo Shanti interpret these laws more strictly than do other groups.

According to one of their own publications:

a. On the first day of issuing (monthly period) is counted as day one, a red flag must be at the gate.

b. Empress [Bobo Shanti woman] must separate herself from the Kingdreds [men] of the family and must not be *seen or heard* (emphasis mine) until the 21st day, the end of purification.

c. In the time of separation all windows in free view must be closed....

i. While on monthly vacation [!] Empress must not leave the Courts unless it's an emergency; if there is an emergency the Royal International Guard must be notified, and the Empress must be covered when leaving the Court....

n. An Empress that is not unclean (free) [not menstruating] would not stay with one that is unclean (Ethiopia Africa Black International Congress, n.d.).

Bobo Shanti women say that they welcome these respites, since it gives them a reprieve from household duties. Some women from other groups also indicated that they accepted these constraints.

A Nyabingi woman put it this way:

[A] Rasta principle is when you're getting your period. You mustn't do anything for the king man [spouse]. Not just your own [king man], you know, but all the bredren for seven days because you're unclean. It is the period of purification.

The importance of rules of pollution go far beyond respite from household duties. To deem women as polluted based on regularly occurring biological functions is to insult their very existence. Moreover, this monthly containment automatically precludes their participation in other spheres of society.[1] In addition to women not being able to become preachers based on their biology, neither can they attend religious ceremonies during menses or attend other social events. Since women are considered polluted dur-

---

1. While women in many other religious groups in Jamaica are not forbidden from cooking or socializing with other "free" members of society, research conducted by Chevannes (n.d.) clearly indicates that a large proportion of men of all religious affiliations think that they should not have sex with a woman while she is menstruating. Some men also feel that during this period they should have sexual relations with another woman.

ing their menstruation and seven days before and after, their participation in every-day activities is limited to nine or ten days out of every month. Thus, women's biology is used systematically to institutionalize their marginalization in political and socio-cultural arenas.

Frantz Fanon presents a keen analysis on the interaction of the material and cultural aspects of colonialism and the way that they are mutually reinforcing. He suggests that it is insufficient for the colonizer to constrain colonized people physically and materially, but that the colonizer must also debase their culture and morality as well. The role of European religion in reinforcing the autodestruction of African people's culture is clearly stated:

> The Church in the colonies is the white people's Church, the foreigner's church. She does not call the native to god's ways but to the ways of the white man, of the master, of the oppressor.... That is why we must put the DDT which destroys parasites [and] the bearers of disease, on the same level as the Christian religion which wages war on embryonic heresies and instincts, and on evil as yet unborn (Fanon 1968:42).[2]

Detrimental as it was, Christian dogma became well entrenched in African and Diaspora societies and remains the major religion in the Caribbean islands. In Jamaica over ninety-five percent of the people are Christian (Population Census 1991:12) and are avid students of the Bible. Not only has Christianity acted as a fifth column in mollifying the population as a whole, it also constitutes the framework around which patriarchal relations have been built. My conversations with Rastafarian women and men revealed ways in which religion acts as a charter for the subordination of women. While many Rasta women do not see themselves as subordinate to men, their lack of personal mobility and their secondary social and cultural status relative to men belie this notion.

Polluted Women in Africa

Women's polluted status in pre-colonial Africa is writ large and sacralized into ritual dogma. Their ostensible worthlessness is defined in terms of their femaleness and their femaleness is equated with pollution.

Rasta women are doubly oppressed because they live not only according to Christian ideology, but are entrenched in African cultural mores that have traditionally subordinated women. Although several scholars (e.g, Sudarkasa 1987) contend that in pre-colonial African societies women were "equal" to men, this claim requires closer inspection. The status of African women as second-class citizens is evident in social and political

---

2. Brilliant as Fanon was, he did not address the issue of women in colonized societies.

spheres and is reified by a cultural framework that legitimates their subordination. In the social arena, women's mobility and sexuality are clearly controlled by men.

In pre-colonial African societies women's initiation ceremonies were controlled by men who also participated in these rituals. This is noteworthy since male rituals were strictly the purview of men and any woman who dared to look at any part of these services was subject to severe punishment, even death. The secrecy that surrounds male rituals mystifies men's status and confers upon them an aura of sacredness and greatness. Not only are female ceremonies more public, but they are predicated on their ostensible polluted status which acts to galvanize male superiority and male purity.

Some of the more critical studies of African societies clearly point to the ritual consolidation of male power (Brain 1978; Hafkin and Bay 1976:1–18; Henn 1986). Brain (1978:180) describes puberty rites among the Luguru of Tanzania where young girls are obliged to remain in seclusion for one or more years. During this period, they must attend to gourd dolls, allow themselves to be sexually fondled by males, and although not allowed to wash, they are expected to hide any signs of menstrual blood (Brain 1978:180). Clearly, female initiation is an initiation into their subordinate status as women. Luguru girls are taught to

> take care of sweeping and cleaning; never refuse your husband; use three pieces of cloth to wipe him after intercourse and keep them washed; do not commit adultery; when you menstruate dig the blood into the ground and never climb into the loft for food at that time...; mothers must not teach their daughters; don't be stubborn, especially with your husband, stubborn ones die of snakes (Swantz 1965:5–6).

Brain (1978:184–186) suggests that the circumscription of women derives from male jealousy. In order to counteract their power of procreation, women are deemed polluted and therefore not as worthy as their male counterparts. This assigned polluted status lays the groundwork for a number of beliefs and practices that further undermine women's control over their own bodies, full participation in socio-political activities, and access to valuable resources. High on the list of practices that control women's bodies is female genital mutilation (FGM).

While many scholars and non-scholars alike would rather close their eyes to this horrendous practice and explain it away by uttering the seemingly sacred term, "cultural relativity," I suggest that it is more humane to open up discussion rather than ignore this centuries-old practice. Both Muslim and non-Muslim African societies in many parts of Africa mutilate the genital organs of young girls by removing the clitoris, labia minora, and/or labia majora. There are a number of myths that act to perpetuate this practice, which, in most societies, is also condoned by women.

Women participate in their own subordination and internalize a panoply of beliefs that legitimate FGM and ensure male control over their bodies and their sexuality. Among these are the beliefs that if a woman is not "circumcised,"

- the clitoris will grow like a penis and hang between the legs if it is not removed.
- the woman will remain childless if she is not excised.
- the clitoris is an evil, which makes men impotent and kills children at birth.
- it frightens the men and destroys crops (Walker and Parmar 1993:139–140).

These beliefs are effective because they are inculcated from the very beginning of females' lives. Moreover, like all myths, they articulate and support already existing institutions that are central to the survival of particular social and political structures.

Since most African societies are dependent on a successful harvest for survival, few women would want to be held responsible for the failure of a year's crop. In addition, since African women's worth is defined in terms of their ability to produce many children, neither are they willing to be held responsible for childlessness.[3] When young girls grow up in a cultural milieu where these beliefs are embedded, they are not able to easily question them.

Girls endure inordinate pain and disease as a result of FGM. FGM is usually performed under unsanitary conditions and often results in infections, incontinence, and even death. After the operation, girls are sewn up, leaving only a small hole the size of a straw for the elimination of urine and blood. In spite of these sequelae, these practices persist so that men can maintain control over women.

Polygyny as Sexual Control

Polygyny is another practice that is endemic to African societies in precolonial Africa. While many scholars propose that polygyny facilitates agricultural production, this explanation is far from adequate since it does not explain why other forms of community organization could not be uti-

---

3. Actually the myth connecting female genital mutilation with childlessness demonstrates how little control women have in African societies since even circumcised women who are fertile are blamed if they do not become pregnant. Men's egos will not allow them to consider that it may be their own infertility that is at fault.

lized for the same purpose. Neither does it explain why women would not marry two or more men towards the same end.

In actuality, polygyny is nothing more than men controlling sexual and domestic access to women. Pollution also enters into this multi-partner relationship since women are considered especially polluted when they are menstruating. Given that they cannot engage in sexual activity during these periods, it follows that men *must* have access to more partners for their continued sexual pleasure.

From the beginning, polygyny has also been a part of some Rastafarians communities. Those who consider it their right to spread their seed as far as possible also expect women to be faithful to their mates.

In African societies men also capitalize on women by virtue of the bride price. Men who are members of the wife's family of orientation also benefit in a material sense from the prizes they receive during the marriage process. In pre-colonial and contemporary societies girls are often promised to men well before they reach puberty. The actual marriage is sealed with a bride price that might be in the form of money, cattle, or other commodities. Girls and women have very little, if any, say in this whole affair and are used as pawns in the consolidation of ties between male members of the two families. As Gayle Rubin states,

> If it is women who are being transacted, then it is men who give and take them who are linked, the woman being a conduit of a relationship rather than a partner to it (1975:174)

The derogation of African women is also made clear in the literature written by continental Africans. In Buchi Emecheta's *Bride Price* (1976) it is clear from the very beginning that girls are born for the benefit of boys and men. At a very young age, the main protagonist, Aku-nna, is expected to perform household chores on a routine basis while her brother spends his time playing outside. As she approaches puberty, her worth is equated with how large a bride price she can fetch. When her mother, Ma Blackie, becomes widowed she goes into seclusion for nine months, wears ragged clothes, and leaves her hair uncombed and disheveled in order to demonstrate her worthlessness without a husband. The fact that Ma Blackie is obliged to marry her brother-in-law is yet another example of the lack of choices available to African women.

We see other examples of the derogation of African women in Chinua Achebe's, *Things Fall Apart* (1976). Okonkwo considers it fitting to beat one of his wives because his dinner is not ready when he arrives home. This and other examples from African literature indicate that violence against women was common in pre-colonial societies. Amina Mama (1996) presents a number of contemporary accounts where women are mutilated or killed by their male partners. One example will suffice.

A Kenyan man decided to gouge out his wife's eyes because she did not bear him any male children. In many parts of Africa, if a woman only bears daughters, she is considered childless (Mama 1996). The savage and viscious nature of assaults against women is alarming in and of itself, but what is equally shocking is that violence against women in Africa often goes unpunished—a scenario that is redolent of violence against women worldwide (Russell, D. 1992; Singer 1992; Bart 1993; Bopp and Verdalis 1987).

African men are joined by men around the world who routinely visit violence against women. Christian dogma, as well as customary beliefs, legitimate these behaviors. Women also play a role in the perpetuation of violence since many accept their subordinate status which allows for their perpetual subjugation.

Chapter 7

Cultural Ideology and RastafarI Women

In addition to the Rastafarian tenets already discussed, Rastafarians also engage in other practices that set them apart from the rest of the Jamaican populace. Many Rastafarians abstain from eating meat and subject themselves to other dietary restrictions. These constraints have been motivated by a belief in natural foodways and are supported by Biblical scriptures. In addition to food differences, Rastas have also developed a language which they integrate with normal Jamaican speech, and one which they believe better accommodates their belief systems. In many cases Rastas are also physically distinguishable from other Jamaicans based on their dress and hair.

Rasta Language (I-Man)

Rastafarians add new prefixes to words, wholly create new words, and give different meanings to the existing lexicon. Rastas are sensitive to English words and sounds that have negative connotations: for example, the sin in sincerely is changed to incerely or icerely. Similarly "ded" in dedicate is redolent of "dead", and is changed to levicate. Other words in this category include downpressor for oppressor, and downstroy for destroy.

Rastas habitually use the "I" (from Haile Selassie "I") and pronounce it the way North Americans would pronounce the first person singular "I." Often they replace the first letter or syllable of words using "I." A few examples are "Ital," meaning vital (or natural) and usually refers to natural food. "Irie" is another Rasta term meaning "cool" or "alright" and one which has been adopted by many other Jamaicans and non-Jamaicans.

The term "I and I" or, more accurately "I 'n I" is used to refer to the first person singular or in place of "you." One "I" represents the person speaking and the other "I" refers to the god that lives within the self. Forsythe (1983), a Rastafarian writer, discusses the meaning of "I 'n I", and states that

> [t]he little I or me refers to the lower self of man, to his body and its ego, that part of him which is born and will die... The Big I is the everlasting,

immortal or "true" self that was never born and can never die. It is the spirit of divinity and holiness residing in the depth of each (Ibid:85).

As indicated by Pollard (1994:6), scholars have differed on their understanding of the meaning of "I n I." These different views notwithstanding, what is more important is the perceived need on the part of Rastafarians to create a language that reflects their own vision of reality. The term "I-man" is particularly interesting for our purposes here since it is a term meaning "I," but one that can only be used to refer to men.

Other words in the Rasta Iyaric glossary include:

Irate:	Crete
Icall:	Recall
Iceive:	Receive
Iclare:	Declare
Iditate:	Meditate
Itation:	Meditation

Rasta also have a lexicon of other words that are created from existing usage such as livity (way of life), livit (diet) and overstand (understand). Such conversions factor out the negative connotations ostensibly implicit in their original form. This conversion of the standard language is typical of groups who seek to set themselves apart from the rest of society. As indicated above, Rastas have organized themselves in such a way that would preclude their alliance with the masses of African people. Creating a specific language that is based on the divinity of Selassie I widens this chasm.

Ital Food

Food beliefs and practices also distinguish Rastafarians from the larger population (Lake 1985). In general, they advocate a philosophy that repudiates processed foods. Their focus on natural foods emanates from their emphasis on living according to African tradition and from a strict interpretation of the Bible. Although some Rastas have a great deal of flexibility in their diet, some adhere strictly to food rules.

Rastas emphasize eating food that is in its natural, unprocessed state. Some are vegetarians and practice all types of vegetarianism from vegan to lacto-ovo.[1] Others do not consume milk because they incorrectly believe that it is not consumed in Africa (Landman-Bogues 1976). Other foods

---

1. A segment of the Rastafarian population is vegetarian and may observe any one of the following vegetarian regimes.

Lacto-Ovo	Consume no animal flesh but include eggs and dairy products.
Ovo	Consume no animal flesh and no dairy products, but do consume eggs.
Vegan	Consume no animal flesh and no eggs or other dairy products.

and beverages that some Rastas avoid, at least theoretically, include cheese, white flour products, and alcoholic beverages. Some Rastas also believe that they should only consume "air foods," i.e., foods that are not grown underground. The origin of this belief is not clear, but it does not appear to be one that will endanger their health status since carbohydrates, vitamins A, and C found in most root foods are readily available from other sources. Other foods that are forbidden by some members who follow strict dietary guidelines include the following:

Meat
Fish   Alcoholic Beverages
Salt   Rum
Eggs   Beer
Sardines   Stout
Bully Beef   Wine
Ham   Brandy
Bacon   Gin
Chicken
Cheese   No Processed Beverages, e.g.
Patties   Milk
                            Horlick
White Flour Products   Ovaltine
Buns   Milo
Bread   Cocoa
Cake   Coffee
Dumplings   Soda
Gravy

   While Rasta proscriptions around food are discussed in much of the literature (Nicholas 1979:61; Landman-Bogues 1976), I want to emphasize that food rules are often relaxed. The vast majority of Rastas may not deal with alcohol, pork, or beef, but many members will eat all manner of other foods, even if the food is processed. Necessity often takes precedence over dietary proscriptions.
   Some Rastafarians go through a fasting period that lasts from March 1 through Good Friday. The Bobo Shanti in Bully Bay indicated that they did not impose this restriction on children. Studies concerning child nutrition in Jamaica have not found that malnutrition is more prevalent among Rastas than in the Jamaican child population in general. Rastafarian infant feeding practices may even be superior.
   My fieldwork in 1984 revealed that Rastafarian women are more likely to breast feed their children and do so for a longer period of time than

---

Fruitarian   Consume no animal flesh, eggs, or dairy. Also exclude grains and
                vegetables from their diet.

other women in Kingston. These findings were based on a small sample of thirty Rasta women and thirty non-Rasta women who were used as controls. Fifty percent of the Rastafarian mothers breast fed their children for four or more months, compared to forty-three percent of the non-Rasta mothers. This difference is not statistically significant; however, it was significant that more Rastafarian mothers were committed to breast feeding their infants with the addition of supplements than members of the control group. This is even more remarkable given that Rasta mothers in this sample were better educated and more likely to be employed than non-Rastas. Although the sample size in this study was too small to suggest that cultural identity was the cause of breast feeding practices, there was a strong indication that Afrocentric orientation had a positive effect on attitudes about and the duration of breast feeding.

Hair and Headdress

Just as Europeans exploited African land and labor, they also undermined their cultural economies. During the period of enslavement, Africans in the west were forbidden from speaking their own languages, from playing their own music, and continuing their kinship patterns. These proscriptions created a deep chasm between Africa and the Diaspora, but none as deep as the self-hate created by the idea that African physical bodies were somehow less worthy than that of Europeans. Europeans vilified African skin color, physiognomy, and hair.

The most devastating aspect regarding the derogation of the African body is that a large percentage of Africans themselves have internalized these views. As discussed in a number of works (see e.g., Isaacs 1964; Jones 1994; Lorde 1986; White and White 1995) negative values placed on the African body were introduced and proliferated during the slave era. These ideas continue into the present. That diaspora Africans have a negative attitude toward natural African hair texture is witnessed by the large percentage of people who have straightened or otherwise processed their hair. The negative language used to describe natural hair and negative attitudes directed toward women with natural hair is also evidence that African hair texture is devalued.

Almost all diaspora Africans beyond the age of five (perhaps even younger) understand the concept of "good" hair and "bad" hair. Hair is thought to be good if it approximates European hair in straightness (grade) or curliness. If a person has kinky African hair, many people of African descent refer to it as "bad" hair. Along with negative views regarding hair, dark skin is also considered by many to be a badge of inferiority (Russell, Wilson, and Hall 1992; Rushing 1988). I have written more extensively on these issues elsewhere (see Lake 1998).

In spite of ample evidence to the contrary, many people contend that Caribbean peoples are free from the problems of racism and color stratification that exist in the United States. In fact, colonialism and capitalism have had the same effect all over the Diaspora, differing from place to place only in particulars. Just as in the United States, European slave owners in Jamaica gave freedom and other privileges to their mulatto offspring. Darker skinned Caribbeans internalized the European value that "lighter was somehow better." "Good" hair was also at a premium.

While this cultural and racial hierarchy was true for women and men, women were more closely compared to and evaluated in terms of European beauty standards. Still today, in order for African descended women to be considered feminine and beautiful, they are encouraged to straighten their hair in order to approximate European models. For women especially, by maintaining their natural hair texture, they are exhibiting their Africanness which for centuries has been devalued based on European standards of beauty.

African men, whether their hair is straightened or not—are stereotyped as super virile. Thus women and men of African descent are derogated based on their *being* African. Women bear a double burden since many men of African descent have also internalized the notion of superior European female beauty and expect women of African descent to follow this model.

Most people of African descent around the world, including in Africa, are straightening, gheri curling, or otherwise transforming their hair. As a group, Rastas are exceptional in this regard since they revel in the glory of their natural African crown. From their own accounts, they let their hair grow long and do not comb it, preferring to leave it totally in its natural state.

Although this may be true for some Rastas, it is clear that others, even though they let their hair lock and maintain its natural African texture, regularly groom their hair in a variety of lengths and styles. According a 1960 report by Smith, et al., hair treatment falls within three categories. "Locksmen" refers to those

> whose hair is matted and plaited and never cut, neither their beards; the Beardmen, who wear their hair and beards but may trim them occasionally and do not plait the hair.... Both these groups wear moustaches. Thirdly there is the Baldhead or 'cleanfaced' man who is not obviously distinguishable from the ordinary Jamaican except by some article such as the yellow, green and red pompon or scarf. Cleanfaced men are mostly employed (Ibid:25).

It is interesting to note that this passage describes dreadlocks in terms of men. A small sampling of the variety of male hair styles is depicted in the photos on page 108.

The original impetus for Rastafarians to lock their hair has been a matter of much debate. Some Rastas have reported that they began to grow

Figure 4. Male Dreadlocks

Figure 4. Male Dreadlocks

dreadlocks in the fashion of Masai warriors. Mansingh and Mansingh (1985:109) suggest that Rastafarians began wearing dreadlocks as a result of seeing East Indian indentured servants and holy men in Jamaica who wore their hair in this fashion. They also assert that Joseph Hibbert, one of the original Rasta leaders, referred to locks as Jagavi or Jatavi which are Hindi terms. While it is possible that Rastas may have borrowed from Hindi aesthetics, it is also likely that they fashioned their hair after African styles. The origin is less important than their impetus to follow the dictates of the Bible (discussed below) and to set themselves apart from the rest of Jamaican society. Their attribution of this practice to ancient Africa is telling.

In one of his recent works, Chevannes (1995:77-126) suggests that the first group of Rastafarians to wear dreadlocks was a group of young dissident Rastas known as the Youth Black Faith (YBF) which emerged in 1949. According to Chevannes, this group consisted of younger Rastafarian converts who were interested in changing the revivalist practices within the organization. It is Chevannes' contention that the YBF's impetus for wearing dreads did not emerge from East Indian prototypes or, as suggested by Campbell (1990:96), from images of Masai warriors, but from a desire to be viewed as deviants.

Before Rastas emerged on the scene there were homeless men who roamed the streets with long, unkept hair that was essentially the same as dreadlocks worn today. They were unkept in hair, dress, and cleanliness and were regarded as outcasts by the rest of Jamaican society. The Youth Black Faith adopted this shocking style in order to similarly and intentionally distance themselves from the rest of Jamaican society. This practice is similar to that adopted in the early 1930s when Rastafarian men wore beards to more closely associate themselves with Haile Selassie and to distinguish themselves from the general populace. Even though there were women RastafarI since the beginning of the organization, the group was often referred to as "bearded men, the beards or beardmen" (Chevannes 1995:98).

Homiak (1995:127-181) differs in his account of the origins of dreadlocks and asserts that the Youth Black Faith kept their hair cut and groomed and did not wear beards. He put the date of wearing dreadlocks in the 1950s when young males came into the organization after the Youth Black faith. He suggests that "the prior generation (exemplified by the Youth Black Faith) entered Rasta as Combsomes and later became Dreadlocks (1995:134). Homiak (1985:183-185) recounts portions of an interview with Sister Merriam Lennox, an elder Rastafarian woman, who describes the splits over hair culture that took place in the 1950s.

> At dat time in Abacka (Back-o-Wall) man spring up dem own different kinda Rasta...different Rasta was still existing...[but] is only after de (1958) Convention close date we have the springing up of de Nyabinghi Order. Dis is when de Locks-Dread...come right up. We (older Rastas) were talking of de Coptic House when dem man come and 'low-rate' Coptic.
>
> Those ancient bredrin (from before the Convention), some a dem 'fall dong' (leave Rasta), some a dem pass off, some still ina demself. Still, plenty of de old time Rastaman couldn't tek de mesage of de Locks-Dread Nyahman...couldn't tek de message!

Whatever the origins of this practice, it is clear that it fit well within Rasta's African cosmology. The fact that there are Africans who wear their hair in dreads was enough to validate the practice.

Even though Rasta women and men wear dreadlocks it is only women who are admonished to cover their hair. This practice is partially based on Christian dogma that admonishes women to wear a head covering to hide their beauty, which is also seen as their shame. The shame, of course, emanates from their being a woman.

> Wives, submit yourselves unto your husbands, as unto the Lord. For the husband is the head of the wife, even as Christ is the head of the church: and he is the saviour of the body. Therefore as the church is subject unto Christ, so let the wives be to their own husbands in every thing (Ephesians 5:22-24)
>
> But I would have you know, that the head of every man is Christ; and the head of the woman is the man; and the head of Christ is God. Every man praying or prophesying, having his head covered, dishonoureth his head. But every woman that prayeth or prophesieth with her head uncovered dishonoureth her head: for that is even all one as if she were shaven.

> For if the woman be not covered, let her be also shorn: but if it be a shame for a woman to be shorn or shaven, let her be covered. For a man indeed ought not to cover his head, forasmuch as he is the image and glory of God: but the woman is the glory of the man. For the man is not of the woman; but the woman of the man. Neither was the man created for the woman; but the woman for the man (I Corinthians 11:3-9).

The vast majority of Rasta women take these passages seriously and routinely cover their hair in public. A sampling of head coverings is presented in the photos to the right.

The Bobo Shanti are distinguishable mainly by their dreadlocks and sometimes by red, black, green, and yellow turbans. Men can choose whether to cover their hair or to go bare headed, but women are expected to always cover their hair in public. As indicated by the photographs on page 112, even though most Rasta women accept these proscriptions, there are a few who move to a different drummer. One of the most outspoken and independent Rastafarian women that I know offered the following:

> If I feel like wearing my locks out, I wear them out. But if I feel like wearing a head thing I wear it. When I feel like wearing European clothes I wear it. At the end of the day, I'm not fighting for equal opportunity with nobody. Equal to who? I'm fighting for my freedom. And the first step to freedom is freedom of choice.

Cross-Cultural Markers of Inferiority

In all societies clothes are used as markers that connote economic status, gender, and sexuality (among others). For example, in *Veiled Sentiments* Abu-Lughod (1986) focuses on ways that Bedouin women communicate their social and sexual availability with various articles of clothing. Indeed, the transition from being single to being married is marked by a change of clothing. After the marriage is consummated, the woman's apparel includes "two critical pieces: the black headcloth that doubles as a veil and the red woolen belt" (Ibid:134). The red belt symbolizes her femaleness and fertility.

The black veil always accompanies the red belt in this society. Bedouin men wear head coverings, but they are not obliged to wear a belt that would symbolize their fertility. Bedouin women do not cover their entire faces with their veils, but wear it in a variety of ways and circumstances to communicate respect and sexuality.

Abu-Lughod argues that veiling is not done to prevent sexual interest, but to indicate "shame of sexuality." The veil represents a woman's distance from sexuality in general and, concomitantly, her respect for social order. It is also important to emphasize that these women do not wear the veil out of respect for other women, but in deference to men who they consider to be higher in the social hierarchy. Essentially, women wear the veil for those

Figure 5. Rasta Women with Head Coverings

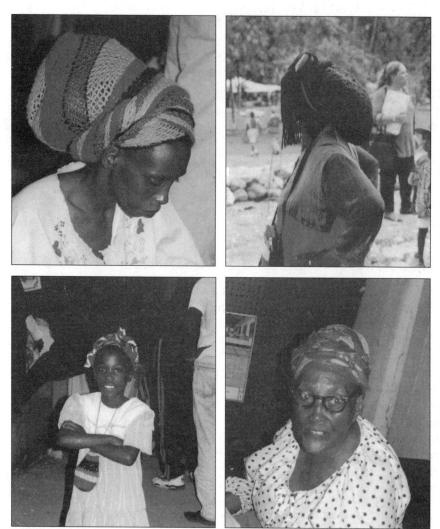

who have authority over them (Ibid:163). In so doing, they pay homage to and perpetuate their own subordination. Macleod (1991:125-141) suggests that the ankle length skirts and veils worn by Bedouin women demonstrate that they are righteous and deserving of respect. This view raises the obvious question, which is why women are not deserving of respect without these accouterments?

In spite of the fact that men require no such symbols as markers of their status, several contemporary scholars claim that this garb gives women power

Figure 6. Rasta Women without Head Covering

(Macleod 1991:125-136). Such views lead one to believe that some women have accepted oppression as a given and are helpless to change the structure that confines them. Macleod contradicts her own assertion when she states that "*higab* (veils) can protest and ameliorate women's situation ... by ... encompassing traditional values of honor, virtue, and dignity" (1991:133). Veiling, however, ... [conveys] protest but also symboliz[es] women's need to acquiesce and accommodate to the existing structure of power relations (Ibid:137).

A return to "tradition" does not empower women, but further submerges them to the will of men. By covering their bodies in extreme ways, women are seen as adhering to three basic principles. The first is that women's dress is controlled by men. It is interesting that in Muslim (Watson 1973), Rasta, and other societies there appears to be little discussion about controlling men's behavior or their dress. If women do not wear the veil, then, according to advocates of this practice, it is *they* who are the instigators of sexual harassment. Lastly, it is clear that women are not viewed as dignified and virtuous in and of themselves. This is the underlying issue, which, if placed on the table, would upset a panoply of myths and attitudes about women which relegates them to a polluted status.

Physical markers are necessary codes that inscribe social messages across women's bodies. As Douglas (1970:71) states

> bodily control is an expression of social control.... There is little prospect
> of successfully imposing bodily control without the corresponding social
> forms. And lastly, the same drive that seeks harmoniously to relate the
> experience of physical and social, must affect ideology.

Indeed, one of the essential characteristics of oppression is that the oppressed population must be easily identifiable (Turner 1984:). While women would in any case fit this criteria, the clothes they wear and how they wear them are used as badges that stamp their inferiority in very specific ways. Prescriptions for women's clothing do not end with head coverings, but extend to their entire bodies.

With the exception of Bobo Shanti men who sometimes wear long robe-like covering over their pants, most Rastafarian men dress the same way as other Jamaican men. Almost all Rasta women wear long skirts or dresses and head coverings. Some of the women wear pants but stipulate that they must not be tight fitting, made out of African print, and cut in an African style. All Rasta women stated that their dress is symbolic of their difference from other women.

Rasta women's dress, like other aspects of their belief system, is predicated on Biblical interpretations.

> The woman shall not wear that which pertains to a man, neither shall a man put on a woman's garment: for all that do so *are* [emphasis in original] abomination unto the LORD thy God (Deuteronomy 22:5).

Given the internalization of Biblical rhetoric most Rasta women spoke positively about their dress code.

> When you see a Rasta dawta come, you know she's a Rasta because of the way she adorns herself. We no wear pants, we no wear shorts, you know. In the good old ancient way, that's the way we dress.

Another Rasta women has similar opinions about the meaning of Rasta women's dress.

> People look up to you for certain things. Like in my community, everybody looks up to me. They wouldn't expect me to walk around bear headed or without sleeves.

Another informant avers that long dresses are the mark of morality which gains them respect.

> Rasta women have a certain dignity, the way they dress and the way they speak and the way they walk in such a dignified way. You'd never see a Rasta woman dye her hair six different colors and wearing some little thing. It's a total consciousness. So we are seen as more of a moral people in terms of keeping the sanity of the flesh on a low profile. Yes. That is how we as a people gain respect from society.

While this woman lauded the dress ethic of Rastafarian women, she also thought that some of the proscriptions were unnecessarily restrictive.

> I'm one of the women who likes to wear my hair without a tie and you
> might find that the [Rasta] sisters have a problem with that. So others who
> are radical like me might defend it and say, "No, she's a Rasta because she
> do this and she do that. Just what Rasta is about." Because we are about
> development and progress, yes. And being a Rasta is one of the highest
> forms that you should definitely try to promote in terms of His Majesty
> [Haile Selassie] because he's a progressive man. He speaks of development,
> that we should develop ourselves so that our race can be strong. So I might
> put beads in my hair and somebody might have problems with that. A
> Rasta woman might say that I shouldn't decorate my hair, but that's just her
> concept. Because whether you wear it on your hair or on your neck or
> ankle, it's no different because each part of you is important. My hair is as
> important as my neck. So you get different people's views. You just have to
> live and be satisfied deep down within yourself and know what you want.

This passage is indicative of the fact that Rasta culture, like all cultures,
is not static, but in a constant state of dynamic change. This more radical
stance might indicate that changes are occurring among Rasta women,
but I suggest that these changes may not outpace gender-based codes in
the rest of Jamaican society.

The Linguistic Containment of Women

Language is the symbolic purveyor of culture. It not only allows us to
express ideas and values, but is the foundation upon which they are built.
Ways in which language, as part of a panoply of other symbols, has sus-
tained male privilege and the derogation of women in all societies points
to the pivotal position of this medium. The language of sexism, much like
the language of racism, relegates women to the status of children or second class citizens. Since this language is so regularized in our every-day
speech, we hardly notice how it "reflects the 'superiority' of the male and
the 'inferiority' of the female, resulting in a master-subject relationship"
(Bosmajian 1992:341). Examples of this hierarchal use of language is
replete in all societies. Let me suggest a few examples.

In many African societies there is no word for she, he being the pronoun that represents all human beings. While there is a pronoun that represents females in European societies, often the male pronoun is used to represent both sexes. Likewise, "mankind" represents humankind, "man"
represents women and men. Moreover, the ordering of words, such as,
men and women, boys and girls, he and she, gives primacy to males. The
commonality of this usage has had the effect of institutionalizing images
of women as secondary or non-existent. While many people hasten to suggest that this "generic" language does not have any deleterious effects or
malintent, reactions to biased language when it is inverted tells another

story. If, for example, "womankind" replaced "mankind," I suggest that many people would have to rethink the "generic" argument.

Another way that men advance their own image and their credibility is by exercising their privilege of using language more often in public spaces. Looking at the entire span of African and Diaspora African movements, including Civil Rights movements (Burks 1993:71-83), it has been men who have assumed the roles of spokespersons, even though women serve as the footsoldiers in these organizations. Among Jamaican Rastafarians, in all but a few arenas, men are the spokespeople for the entire group. They reinforce their privilege by exploiting the performative aspect of language while at the same time silencing women.

Rastafarians also have a unique way of referring to females and males. Among the Bobo Shanti men are often referred to as "priests" or "prophets." Girls may be referred to as "princesses" and boys are called "princes." Adult women can be referred to as "empresses." Rastafarians as a whole sometimes use the term "queen" to refer to women and "king" or "kingman" for men. Although "queen" is a term that is available, it is rarely used in everyday exchanges, which is not the case for "kingman." Moreover, to the degree that it is used, it exemplifies how women are deified in the abstract and derogated in reality.

Several of my informants remarked that the term most often used to refer to women is "daughter" (or "dawta"). Using the term "daughter" to refer to women relegates them to the status of children, subordinated, once again, to the adult male "kingman." Ironically, the language of Rastafarī is considered by some to be a language of resistance. In order to arrive at such a conclusion, the status of women must be factored out of the picture.

Chapter 8

Misogyny in Caribbean Music

Language as expressed in music reifies how women are perceived and how they perceive themselves. Every-day parlance as well as music lyrics are significant because they reflect people's conceptions of reality. Music lyrics are particularly important to consider since most people rarely analyze them for their political content, especially not in terms of women's status.

Politically, much of popular Caribbean music is either devoid of any practical utility in effecting positive social change, or serves to reinforce negative values and images associated with women and other oppressed sexual minorities. It is important first to separate these two arguments. The first, that reggae is not a revolutionary tool, neither in and of itself nor as an agent of political transformation, is of primary importance. While various forms of Diaspora African music have challenged the status quo, they have not provided the impetus for a new social order. The inability of reggae to put into action the words of rebellion, in addition to its almost universal acceptance by both the oppressors and the oppressed, makes it suspect in terms of its ability to pose any real threat to colonial and neo-colonial regimes. The dangers inherent in wholesale subscription to reggae and other forms of Caribbean music and the belief in their power to release frustrations and revolutionary energies will be explored in greater detail in the following sections.

The second argument, that much of Caribbean music is debilitating to women, homosexuals, and others already holding weakened physical and political positions within society, may be argued in parallel with the initial point that of some Caribbean music is anti-revolutionary.

Throughout the twentieth century various forms of Caribbean music have reflected the uneven relations between women and men (Senior 1991:167–168; Elder 1968:33). Even though reggae is the craze among audiences worldwide, it is rife with negative messages regarding women. This reification of women's subordination in Jamaica did not emerge with the sounds of Shabba Ranks and other reggae artists, but are integral to Caribbean musical culture. It is instructive to look at the similarities among a few musical forms within and outside of Jamaican culture relative to their focus on political-economic issues including their treatment of women. This approach historically situates reggae and points out how women's subordination is intricately woven into the socio-cultural milieu. My argument here is not that Caribbean music itself has created negative attitudes and behaviors toward women, but that it is part of a larger network of misogynist institutions that have shaped long-standing cultural beliefs and behaviors.

Calypso was one of the first forms of popular music that drew on social and economic inequities for its politically conscious message. The roots of calypso, for example, go back to nineteenth century Trinidad when French settlers inhabited the island. After slavery was abolished in 1834 songs called kalindas were sung in a French patois during stick-fighting competitions, a popular form of entertainment among the working class. At the turn of the century these songs were composed in English, replacing the kalinda quatrain with an eight-line verse of calypso. Calypso songs were recorded as early as 1912 but began to proliferate in the 1930s. In the 1940s and 1950s, calypsonians such as Attila and the Lion, Duke of Iron, The Mighty Sparrow, and The Mighty Chalkdust popularized their music in the United States, England, and various parts of Africa and the African Diaspora (Rounder Records Corporation 1990). The effects of the depression and neocolonialism on the island provided sufficient fodder for socially and politically conscious music, as shown in The Mighty Chalkdust's popular calypso song, "The Brain Drain."

> We wasting brain in this our nation —
> Forget party affiliation!
> And we does use we Drain to make we mas:
> Tourist come click-click in photograph —
> All we mas pictures in America...
> Our culture fruits are draining away,
> And we ain't doing nothing to make them stay!
> O yes, we are living on yankee sad songs like bugs...
> This is what I call Brain Drain! (Donnel and Welsh 1996)

Many calypso artists continue to rail against the colonial and neo-colonial governments in Trinidad and in Africa (Warner 1988:53–74). Addressing Europe's hunger for gold in Africa, The Tiger sings,

> Abyssinia appeal to the League for peace
> Mussolini actions were like a beas'
> A villain, a t'ief [thief], a highway robber
> And a shameless dog for a dictator.

Along with these critiques, artists such as The Lion, the Caresser, and Atilla the Hun, address the mounting criminality which evolves out of a sense of hopelessness and the lack of viable alternatives. "We Livin' in Jail" tells such a story.

> Everybody talkin' bout freedom, but it's like everybody blind. If you think we livin' in freedom, then freedom only in your mind. Everywhere I look,

criminals and crook, terrorize us and run amok. We livin' in jail. We livin' in jail. You can't walk the streets no more. You fraid for open your door, like you invitin' war. We livin' in jail. We livin' in jail.

So effective was calypso in capturing local perspectives on the state of Caribbean society that the Trinidadian government exercised censorship authority over musical lyrics. Some songs were even banned from the island. Along with socially conscious music dealing with internal and international events, sexual politics were also grist for calypsonians. Calypso is replete with messages that treat women as worthless human beings, sexual objects, and economic dependents. "Ugly Woman" (Quevedo 1983:50), first sung by Lion, demonstrates how women are only valued as physical beings, and then only if they meet certain standards.

> If you want to be happy and live a king's life
> Never make a pretty woman you wife...
> An ugly woman gives you your meals on time
> and will always try to console your mind
> At night when you lie on your cosy bed
> She will coax, caress you and scratch your head
> And she will never shame her husband at all
> By exhibiting herself with Peter and Paul
> So from a logical point of view
> Always marry a woman uglier than you.

The implication here is clear. The song perpetuates the notion of men controlling women and women deferring to and waiting on men. The lyrics also suggest that an ugly woman will do anything for her man since her ugliness leaves her with no assets at all. The same year "Ugly Woman" was released, Bill Rogers recorded "Ugly or Pretty Woman Paseo" which suggested that it does not matter whether a woman is pretty or not since women, by their nature, will not be faithful to their husbands. As Patricia Mohammed states,

> Whether real or imagined in the milieu in which these calypsonians lived, womanhood is painted with the brush strokes of the biblical Eve in the garden of Eden, capable of great deception of men. Men on the other hand portray themselves as the unwilling victims of a female culture premised on duplicity and cunning, or also capable of guile by using women to satisfy their sexual needs and desire for security (1997).

One calypso hit which emerged in the 1930's has become "legendary in inscribing a model for female sexuality and a prescription for male behaviour in gender relations" (Mohammed 1997:12). "Treat em Rough or Turn em down" condones violence against women and is based on the premise that not only should men physically abuse women, but that women

actually want to be treated in this particular manner[1]. To illustrate the
acceptance of this conceptualization of women, it is interesting to note
that even in a carefully detailed history of calypso (and kaiso) by Quevedo (Attila the Hun), the subject of women or sex does not appear in his historical account (Quevedo 1983).

Ska, Rock Steady, and Reggae

In the 1950s, record producer Clement Dodd encouraged Jamaican
musicians to combine the best of Jamaican mento and African American
rhythm and blues, jazz, and boogie-woogie. The result was a musical
form called ska with accents on the second and fourth beats often moving in a twelve bar blues frame (Davis and Simon 1983:38). Unlike calypso, ska concentrated on lyrics dealing with love rather than social commentary. However, it was similar to calypso in its derogatory treatment
of women. The lyrics in a tune called *Jezebel* by Owen Grey with Clue J
and his Blues Blasters declares a woman, Jezebel, to be "no good" because
she is two-timing a man. This characterization would not be so remarkable if it were not for the fact that in Caribbean societies, it is often acceptable for men to have more than one woman. The term "outside woman"
is commonly used to describe a married man's other woman. But for
Jezebel

> You jus' a foolin' around with another man, Jezebel
> Now I'm all alone
> You can go to hell, Jezebel.

In contrast, rock-steady, another popular musical style of the Caribbean,
focused on issues of hunger and economic marginalization of the masses
of Jamaican people. Purveyors of this music were known as "Rude boys"
whose music was

> vitriolic and sought to challenge authority without demanding a change
> in existing institutional arrangements (Cashmore 1979:10).

Reggae grew out of rock-steady with a message that boldly challenged
the forces of neo-colonialist oppression in Africa and the African Diaspora. While the exact origin of the term "reggae" is unknown, it has been
suggested that the term first appeared in popular usage when in 1968 Toots

---

1. In 1947 another calypsonian Duke of Albany changed the popular chorus to:
   Every now and then cuff them down
   They love you long and they love you strong
   Black up the eye and bruise the knee
   and then they love you eternally (Mohammed 1997:13).

and the Maytals came out with "Do the Reggay," written by Toots Hibbert. According to Hibbert

> Reggae means comin' from the people, y'know? Like an everyday thing. Like from the ghetto. From majority. Everyday thing that people use like food, we just put music to it and make a dance out of it. Reggae means regular people who are suffering, and don't have what they want (Davis and Simon 1977:17).

Reggae has been described as "Jamaican soul music...with accents on the second and fourth beats" (Ibid:12) which has its origins in African and African-Caribbean music. Reggae became popular as a musical form not only because of its unique rhythm, but because it verbalized messages that gave expression to the discontent and rage experienced by many African people around the world. The following discussion calls attention to the positive messages in reggae as well as the problematic representations of women. The focus here is on reggae performed by Rasta and non-Rasta artists.

The spread of Jamaican reggae music to many parts of the world, especially Africa and other parts of the African Diaspora, owes much to the popularity of Bob Marley as a modern-day folk hero (Boot and Goldman 1981). Bob Marley was born on 5 February 1945 on the north side of Jamaica in St. Ann. While still in his teens his mother migrated to the United States. It is during this period that he met Peter Tosh, Bunny Livingstone, and Junior Brathwaite, the trio that would be known as the Wailers. After three unsuccessful albums, Marley and the Wailers scored a hit with *Simmer Down*.

Lyrics that speak to the oppression of people of African descent include tunes such as "Chant Down Babylon" and "Revolution." "Babylon System" from Marley's *Survival* album is unequivocal as to the solution to oppression.

> We refuse to be
> What you wanted us to be.
> We are what we are
> That's the way it's going to be.
> You can't educate I
> For no equal opportunity
> Talking about my freedom
> People freedom and liberty.
> Yeah!
> We've been trodding on the winepress
> Much too long
> Rebel, rebel.

Even though Marley advises the downtrodden to rebel, his message is coupled with surprisingly temperate songs of peace and love. Although not intuitively a contradiction, the potential danger and incompatibility of a missive of peace and love amidst a call to war was a result of a dilution of Marley's revolutionary message that was part of the commercialization of his music.

Diffusion and Defusion of Reggae

Allenye (1994:77) reiterates Garofolo's (1987:77–92) notion that there is a positive relationship between "commodification and ideological appropriation." Importantly, Alleyne states that

> Marley's [texts] are not immune to ideological mediation and defusion by capitalist forces which facilitate their access to discourse (1994:77).

In spite of Marley's charisma and his jargon which challenged international class and race disparities, the fact that reggae has reached global proportions is somewhat of an enigma. Some scholars attempt to explain reggae's widespread appeal based on its

> ...ability to successfully combine both [Western disco rap and funk by] utilizing innovative Western technology while at the same time retaining much of the music's original African flavor, creating a unique blend of both the old and the new (Savishinsky 1994:23).

While all this may be true, it does not explain why other musical genres which have accomplished the same thing, e.g., highlife and calypso, have not met with similar success. These genres created a large market in Africa (Cathcart 1989; Stapleton and May 1987), but not to the degree that reggae has.

Not only has reggae been incorporated into Africa's popular music, but has served as a purveyor of Rastafarĭ among segments of the African population (Savashinsky 1994:26), especially in Ghana, the Gambia, and Nigeria. Even though there are reggae adherents and artists in some of the Francophone countries, reggae has found its largest audiences in Anglophone Africa (Ibid:33–34). Savashinsky even suggests that reggae has promoted cross-cultural and "pan-African awareness and solidarity" (Ibid 27). Given the actual lack of solidarity among African people, I suggest that this stretches the effect of reggae quite a bit and adds to the mystification that surrounds it. While African reggae groups are proliferating, other Africans continue to annihilate hundreds of thousands of their own and other cultural groups in civil warfare. These events belie any claims that propose increased pan-African awareness.

Neither have conflicts within the Diaspora been ameliorated by reggae messages. Rampant violence on the streets of Kingston, spurred by hopelessness of the masses, is one example that clearly contradicts any notions of revolution. The proliferation of Jamaican gangs in the United States also belies the notion that reggae constitutes a revolutionary force against Babylon or a pathway towards harmony among the masses.

The fact that reggae musicians are dependent on the capitalist structure for the production of their music also makes one question its ostensible revolutionary thrust. Given that many people of African descent embrace reggae as a symbol of revolution, I suggest that this devotion compensates for the lack of any real revolutionary organization—on the part of Rastas or anybody else. That is, people of African descent, on the whole, have not organized politically in such a way that would allow them to control their own destinies. While I think it is possible for them to do so, they have not acquired the cultural and political unity that would strengthen their cause. In the absence of an agenda that speaks to self-determination (as in control over the means of production), many people of African descent grab at the symbols of power and revolution without demanding and organizing for substantive change.

So the question remains—why has reggae received such a phenomenal response? It could be argued that the bouncy beat is catchy—creating an almost irresistible impetus to dance and sing along. But while reggae, as music, (versus its social commentary) is good, it could be argued that it is not a *great* music. Of course, one's musical taste is a matter of personal preference, but the pandemic positive reception of reggae is unusual in the numbers of people who embrace it and in the fervor with which they defend its "greatness."

In the few social arenas where people have dared to announce that they "don't like reggae," the response from fans is unlike what one might hear if one had expressed a similar dislike for, let us say, rhythm and blues or jazz. For one to openly admit that they don't like reggae seems worse than admitting that they don't believe in God. The obvious question is why?

Passionate responses to non-adherents lead me to believe that reggae has produced a kind of messianism in its admirers of both African and European descent. For many people reggae is more than just music. For some people of African descent, reggae replaces the real revolution and offers a sense of liberation without true liberty. Real liberation would involve the total dismantling of capitalist and racist institutions. It would involve African people controlling their means of production—something that will not occur in the absence of a pitched battle. No group of people has ever sung itself free. Actually, the fact that so much time and energy is spent defending and grooving to reggae is a clear testimony that there is a great deal of work in other areas that is not being done.

Music is a medium in which African people have always excelled. But it is not enough. Moreover, while some of the language of reggae may be incendiary, much of it is quite conservative. The prime example of this is how one of Marley's more popular songs, "One Love", has been used in tourism commercials for Jamaica. While Marley sings, "Let's get together and feel all right", images of light skinned children and African Jamaican women braiding White women's hair flash across the screen. It is perhaps the ultimate defusion of reggae's revolutionary tendencies that lends to its popularity.

For European descended people and other liberals, reggae may suggest change without any real change at all—the sine qua non of liberalist ideology. Admonishments to "get up, stand up, stand up for your rights" do not suggest how this posture is going to change control over access to valuable resources. Many other reggae recordings focus on romance, peace and love, or a very diluted "revolutionary" ideology. Any quasi revolutionary messages are mediated by European and European American record companies whose goal it is to produce sounds that are amenable to European and European American audiences. This is not to say that reggae artists have not made any artistic achievements. My analysis seeks to call attention to the mystification that surrounds reggae and which misrepresents it as a radical musical form.

As noted in Alleyne's (1994:77) discussion of Bob Marley's music, western capitalist influence has played a major role in "shaping textual material away from its cultural context." Cushman (1991) also points to the positive relationship between the diffusion and defusion of reggae. Audiences, especially those of European descent, have been placated with a diluted form of reggae which they embraced more for its musical appeal than for its political (albeit defused) message. Cushman also suggests that the notion of "cultural appropriation" is troublesome in so far as it suggests that

> "empowered" audiences...subvert the hegemonic work of bourgeois culture industries by reading bourgeois cultural texts in alternative ways (Ibid 20)....An emphasis on the "empowered actor" fails to take into consideration how processes external to the individual shape both the production and reception, and perhaps even the meaning of culture (Ibid:21).

Cushman's profound insights are tempered by his assertion that if reggae had not been tampered with, it would have served a "transformative" role in Jamaica. He proceeds to argue that music in its diluted form will not alter macro structures in society given their repressive nature. I would add to this by stating that, even in full form, any aspect of popular culture, by itself, will not release African Jamaicans from their state of oppression. Reggae lyrics alone, no mater how volatile, will not feed the hungry (and there are many), clothe and house the poor, or heal the sick. Music can be *part* of a truly revolutionary force if other transformative institutions are in place. It is questionable whether reggae has this capacity since, in its present form, it acts as a safety valve to offset revolutionary *action*.

As Cushman suggests (1991) whatever revolutionary potential reggae had has been defused by the capitalist ideologies of the international recording industry. Reggae music has been transformed from the original African Jamaican sound by dubbing more cosmopolitan instruments and sound over original reggae music. Titles and lyrics were also changed. For example, Bob Marley's 1974 album was originally entitled *Knotty Dread*, but was changed to *Natty Dread* by Chris Blackwell, an English person who is head of Island Records, a company that has promoted scores of reggae artists.

> "Natty" had connotations of 'hip' style and being 'fashionable' in white parlance [whereas] 'knotty' implied a sense of uncompromising Rasta militancy and race-consciousness symbolized by the extolling of locks (Jones 1988:65).

Thus, the sound and the text of reggae have been reformulated so that it would feel comfortable for European and European American audiences. In spite of post-modernist arguments that "allow" the masses to empower themselves through cultural artifacts, in fact, what is occurring is the creation of the illusion of power. While Diaspora Africans are grooving to the reggae beat, capitalist industries continue to prosper once again—using Africans as human capital. In this instance, women *and* men are the brunt of European exploitation; however, women are doubly exploited given lyrics which culturally reproduce their sexual objectification. Misogyny within reggae is not surprising; it simply belies the claim that reggae is a medium that promotes revolutionary change.

Repression in the Midst of "Revolution"

While advocates suggest that reggae conveys revolutionary messages (Hebdige 1976:152), many ignore the misogynist ideas that portray women solely as sexual beings, and this, in a subordinate position to men (Campbell 1990:199; Silvera 1980). Women are displayed as sex objects, dependents, housewives, or housewomen.[2] Those who deviate from these roles are maligned as 'slack' and undesirable. Ironically, women are derogated no matter what roles they assume. Research by Anderson and Langley (1988) demonstrates the way in which reggae perpetuates women's roles as housewives and sexual subordinates.

---

2. Anderson and Langely (1988) note that a more appropriate term to describe women who work mostly in the home is "housewoman" and not "housewife" since many women in Jamaica are not wives.

Women who do not elect or reject the role of housewomen are portrayed
as lacking in substance, as shallow, [or] as superficial (Ibid:4).

Even though reggae seems to be the sine qua non of RastafarI there are
some Rasta who reject it altogether. For example, the Bobo Shanti and
the Nyabingi do not embrace reggae. They view it as an undesirable part
of Babylon that does not represent Rastafarian livity. Moreover, there are
Rasta women who find the messages portrayed in reggae music uncom-
plimentary. An example of how some Rasta women and men differ in their
reception of these messages is evident in the following exchange between
a Rasta woman and her partner (Lake 1994).

Rw (Rasta woman) I think the Europeans just want to see the Black race
laughed at according to the things that they promote, things that are not edifying to our young, singing so many derogatory things about women. When
you start to underrate the woman of this world, I think you are doomed.
Rm (Rasta man): I think it's just one aspect of reggae music.
Rw: Yes, but they are playing upon it.
Rm: I think you should tell her [the interviewer] that we still have conscious reggae music whose message hasn't changed from Bob Marley.
Rw: Yah, man, you have that, but what they are promoting now, the most
popular person now in reggae, Shabba Ranks, he's not saying much. He's
even leading the youths astray more than anything else. And you have great
reggae artists who do not gain the popularity because of social status here.
To me I don't see many Rasta women in music and I don't know why because
you have talented Rasta women. I've travelled quite a bit going to different
shows. And of all the shows I've been on, maybe I might be the only Rasta
woman there, sometimes I'm the only woman. I think that's why the music
is getting out of hand because we don't have a lot of women even coming
out and saying that we don't appreciate what they're saying about us.

Mutabaruka, a renowned reggae artist, echoes this sister's sentiments
when he asserted that

[w]hat we have now as reggae music is just a dancing music. It has nothing to do with the mind. Reggae music don't make no sense. They elevate
the music when it attack our women and degrade and downgrade [B]lack
people (Henry 1993:1).

Some of the more positive messages about women have emanated from
women artists during an earlier phase of reggae. Many of these pieces
emerged from *Tuff Gong Records* and Sonia Pottinger's *Hi Tone* studio.
Among the tunes that express Rasta's ideology vis-a-vis women are Rita
Marley's *Who Feels It Knows It* and *Black Woman* by Judy Mowatt. Even
though the lyrics speak to women's burden in slavery and in contemporary society, no mention is made of the male prerogative in and outside of
Rasta society. Lillian Allen is one of the few Rasta sisters who deals direct-

ly with the subject of violence against women in contemporary Jamaican society.

This is exemplified in "Nellie Belly Swelly," a song about a thirteen year old girl who was raped by a man in her garden. The song implies that abuse of females is so common in society that "no sentence was passed on this menacing ass" and it was Nellie who bore the blame for her own victimization. This piece is exceptional since most female Rasta artists sing all praises to Jah (God), the Black man, and Ethiopia. Because misogyny is embedded in Jamaican society at large, many Rastafarian and non-Rasta women artists merely reflect endemic social values and thereby reify the normative order.

In the 1990s women continue to be the main, and often the sole, members of the household who attend to washing clothes, cleaning house, cooking, ironing, and child care. Women are obliged to work just to survive with little time to upgrade their skills or that of their female children. These economic constraints are exacerbated by the cultural validation of these roles in music.

Home T's "She Love the Single Life" derogates women who chose the "single life" over the drudgery of dishes, dirty clothes, and child care. "Duppy Laugh" by Major Mackerel is more explicit on the importance of housewives as domestic servants for their men. Anderson and Langley (1988:4) state that in this song

> one finds a woman who...is celebrated because she possesses the virtues of the domestic or houseperson. She washes, she cooks, she irons his clothes and caters to his every wish—she will even become fat or slim as required. And, in return for the appreciation of her role as house[wife], she even buys him expensive gifts. Men are therefore urged that, if they cannot have the values of beauty and domesticity conjoined in the same women, they should elect one who represents the latter value.

Females are raised to believe that their virtue, as women, lies in their physical bodies. The lyrics in "Duppy Laugh" imply that this woman, who lacks in these virtues, is compelled to do absolutely anything for her mate in order to keep him. Women, themselves, perpetuate these standards in the money and attention they spend on cosmetics and clothes that reveal as much as possible of their physical bodies. The physical body is a beautiful thing to behold and my emphasis on women's attempts to accentuate it does not come from a moral position. The important issue is the motivation behind women's decision to wear tight fitting, flimsy clothes in order to attract a specific man or some imaginary man. Such displays make the statement that what women have to offer is primarily physical. More importantly, the standards of attractiveness are not the same for women and men.

Men can be attractive based on their intelligence, their personality, and their economic position. Women are *only* viewed in terms of what they can do with their bodies, whether it be giving sexual pleasure or doing housework. Men are viewed as more valuable individuals who are not only sexually appealing, but intellectually attractive as well. This dichotomy begins early since girls are raised from the very beginning of their lives to think of themselves as physical objects. At the same time, boys learn just as early they have rights to women's sexuality and to their labor. These messages are reiterated in reggae and other musical forms such as "Hold A Fresh" by Red Dragon, "Wear Yu Size" by Lt. Stitchie and "Two Year Old" by Little John.

Not only are women vilified as women, but Jamaican women are only acceptable if they meet certain standards that are as far as possible divorced from an African woman. "Browning," a song that came out in the early 1990s was a big hit in Jamaica and was just as often heard coming from men's wolf calls on the street as it was on the radio. "Browning" refers to lighter skinned women as being more attractive than their darker skinned peers, a notion that is reflective of the color lines that have historically divided Jamaican society (Richardson 1983; Henriques 1952).

Women's position of dependency is also reified in reggae. "Block Traffic" by Little John is one example among many which suggests that women are not competent to live without men regardless of how the latter treat them. This song suggests that it is a man's place to have as many women (at the same time) as he chooses and that the sooner his women come to terms with this "natural fact," the sooner things will be normalized.

Dance Hall Sexuality

The problems with reggae are repeated and magnified in dance hall music. Shabba Ranks and Buju Banton are good examples of how music is used to reify male supremacy and the inferiority of women. Both depict women in very derogatory ways and explicitly rail against homosexuals. In the videorecording, *The Darker Side of Black*, Gopaul (1994) discusses the effects of reggae and dance hall music on homosexuals and women. The vilification of homosexuality is pertinent to our discussion regarding the derogation of Jamaican women since anti-homosexuality[3] represents the extreme end along a continuum of sexist behavior.

---

3. I use the term "anti-homosexuality" instead of the more commonly used "homophobia" because the latter implies that homophobes are afraid of the homosexuals, when, in fact, what people are afraid of is the abdication of male privilege.

Anti-homosexuality is a key aspect of sexist ideology since it helps to draw sharp boundaries around the definition of how males and females are supposed to behave. For anti-homosexuals, there are no grey areas, there is only black and white. The actual sexuality continuum includes a number of possibilities—asexual, homo, hetero, bi sexual, pan-sexual. Still most people tend to envision sex in very dichotomous terms. Male homosexuals are vilified because they spoil the game that men create and perpetuate. What is at stake is not a dislike or fear of homosexuals (as the term homophobia implies) because of their sexual choices, but men's control over women. Anti-homosexuality is deeply entrenched in Jamaican society and is reified by reggae and dance hall tunes. A few examples will suffice.

> Hug up one another on a feel up leg. Send for an automatic and the uzi instead. Shoot them now come let me shoot them.

"Them," of course, is homosexuals. What Banton was doing, by and large, was recording the attitudes of the vast majority of the Jamaicans. In his "Boom Bye Bye" he also advocates for the annihilation of homosexuals.

> Burn him up bad like an old tyre wheel. Go one Buju Banton you're tough. Boom bye bye in Batty [gay] Boy head. Rude Boy won't promote no Batty boy, they have to be dead.

The use of the term "batty" in Jamaica means "ass" and is almost always used derogatively. The fact that batty has become synonymous with gay is indicative of the institutionalization of anti-homosexuality. In spite of the explicit advocacy of violence in "Boom, Bye Bye," Banton asserts that he has

> heard a number of songs which have incited violence not only against that section of gay people, them, but against Black people as well, you know. And people never went out and truly carried out those actions. But everything is blown out of proportion and God knows why, but there is no way that the wicked can ever prosper (Gopaul 1994).

At the same time that Banton denies that he is inciting violence, he suggests that homosexuals are wicked and proclaims that they must cease to prosper. His lyrics clearly suggest how they should be eradicated.

Even given the worldwide violence perpetrated against this group, Forizelle O'Connor comments in *Darker Side of Black*

> [that Banton] or any one else would [not] expect anybody listening to that song to translate that into actions of harassment against persons who perceive or [who are] known to be homosexuals (Gopaul 1994).

This is a rather peculiar response, especially since O'Connor herself later asserts that if homosexual men were recognized on the street they would be beaten. While it is clear that music lyrics are not the only impetus for violence against homosexuals, it is important to understand the systematic attack on this group, and to see music as an important popular aspect of this repression.

When I visited Jamaica in 1994, a group of homosexuals announced in the press that they were planning a march in downtown Kingston. The response from members of the Jamaican public was that these homosexuals would be stoned if they attempted such a move. Indeed, the anti-homosexuals were lined up in the street, bottles and rocks in hand, awaiting a march that never occurred.

David Dibose, a Jamaican writer living in London, England, relates his personal encounter with violence.

> In terms of my living experience, walking down the streets, I've had to face homophobia which I'd had to face all my life...I've walked down the street faced with physical and verbal abuse, bottles were thrown at me, I was punched. I was kicked. I was pursued for at least twenty yards down the road by at least ten men. They were joined by ten, twenty. I was lying in the middle of the road with my boyfriend being kicked and kicked and kicked as if I were a dog. Nobody raised a hand to help us. Nobody had the decency to ask had we been hurt. Were we alright? Me and my boyfriend were hospitalized [as a result of being beaten] by the people he considered his neighbors and brothers (Gopaul 1994).

Anti-homosexuality is also rampant in other parts of the Caribbean and is sanctioned by the legal system which in many parts of the region considers homosexuals to be criminals (Alexander 1994).[4] Both gay men and women are repressed in Jamaica to the degree that people do not "come out," as such, as some gay people do in many parts of the United States. Nevertheless, people are aware that they exist. Although there are songs which condemn male homosexuals, female homosexuals are rarely discussed in song. The patriarchal ethos in Jamaica is so strong that it is possible that people perceive female homosexuality as insignificant on this island nation. This is not surprising, since many people would like to think that women are *only* attracted to men. The threat of any other prospect is obvious.

Shabba Ranks defends his attacks on gay people by pointing to the Bible and asserting that "God hates homosexuals. Lesbians and gay men ought to be crucified" (Gopaul 1994). It is interesting how Ranks and others choose selectively from the Bible and how the Bible is used as a moral guide, as if written by a god. That is, anti-homosexual behaviors may be

---

4. For a more detailed discussion on responses to homosexuality in Latin America and the Caribbean see Smith, B. (1995); Drucker (1996); and Ferdinand (1996).

motivated by the Bible, but it is important to recognize that the Bible is a text written by male hands in order to draw the lines in bold which separate, and arrange hierarchically, the roles and statuses of women and men. Cornel West cogently argues this dynamic as it exists in all Black nationalist groups.

> What you get in the Black nationalist politics actually is a mirroring of that same kind of patriarchal and homophobic perspective. Why? Because gays and lesbians present a certain kind of alternative to the patriarchal identity that is reinforced by Black nationalist politics. So that...when you hear allusions to Louis Farrakhan and others, what you're hearing on the one hand is positive—Black identity, Black self-love, Black self-affirmation—and something negative—patriarchal identity reinforced, homophobia promoted, and attempts to provide various ways of policing Black folk into one particular homogeneous blob...(Gopaul 1994).

The notion of policing is an important one since it points to one of a myriad of ways in which women are kept in their place. Since it is men who are the primary supporters of women's subordination, men who jeopardize the role of male superiority (i.e., homosexuals) also threaten the status quo.

Women and Dance Hall

Given Jamaica's patriarchal climate, one would expect sexist lyrics emanating from men. Unfortunately, women who have internalized sexist norms add to these negative images. Lady Saw is one such songstress who plays herself and, by association, all other women. "Stab Up the Meat" is the most graphic example.

> Me hear you can grind good and can fuck straight. Stab up me meat, stab up me meat. The big hood that you have a mad gal out of straight. Stab up me meat. Watch ya! The old time gal for jump out (Ibid).

These passages undermine women's individual and social integrity and reinforce sexist ideas and behaviors that persist in other social spheres. We see this behavior repeated by some African American female rap artists. For example, Little Kim and Foxy Brown, see themselves, and are seen by certain others, as empowering themselves based on the presumed desirability of their sexual parts. While these and other women feel that they are in control, the prevalence of physical abuse directed towards women who are beaten, maimed, or killed by their sexual partners, tells a different story as to where the actual power lies. It would appear then that female rappers' ideas of control are little more than posturing since their claims of sexual power only serve to reinforce men's objectification of their physical beings. Moreover, derogatory lyrics that point to women's physical attributes undermine the integrity of women and make good investments for capitalists in the music industry while doing little to enhance the images or the economic condition of women.

Self-deprecating behavior in the dance halls and misogynist music in Jamaica is not the cause of women's secondary status, but constitutes an important factor that reifies sexual subordination. DJ music critic O'Connor presents an opposing viewpoint to those who would applaud women's public sexual displays.

> The content of the DJ music frankly I have found very offensive in so many instances. I would highlight too the way they treat women. I think it is just absolutely unacceptable. I find it, as a proud Black woman, personally offensive. But the professional side of me has to bear in mind the realities and what they are reflecting (Gopaul 1994).

Indeed, what they are reflecting is the emphasis on females as primarily sexual objects. Females are encouraged to demean themselves from very young ages since they are admonished to pay more attention to the development of their physical attributes than their intellectual or emotional capital. They are also given fewer freedoms than boys and are treated as less than second class citizens. They are implicitly and explicitly taught that their place is in the home—serving men.

In light of these realities, it is perplexing how scholars can honor dance hall music and dance hall behaviors that graphically devalue women since this behavior is nothing more than a continuation of women's objectification. Popular culture critic Carolyn Cooper (1993) condones misogynist lyrics as well as women's lascivious behaviors on the dance floor.

> I see the dance hall as the female fertility rite. The female body is the central figure. Men are very much on the periphery. They're on the margins watching women parade.... Some people see this transgression, women going outside the bounds of convention... so this transgressive projection of the body by women I see as something positive—a way of African women asserting the beauty of their bodies in a culture where Black women's bodies are not valued (Gopaul 1994).

Film director, Inge Blackman expresses similar sentiments in Gopaul's film. What is interesting about these views is that it is very unlikely that either Cooper or Blackman would ever appear scantily dressed, performing sexual shows like the women they describe. Moreover, Cooper's analysis of the issue of sexism is extremely narrow since it does not address the fact that most people see women *only* in terms of their bodies. Behaving in extremely sexual ways—often to attract men—does nothing to alter this fact.

What I find most interesting about the whole affair is that dance hall antics are nothing new. Women have been undressing for men in theaters and bars for centuries—the more they take off, the more they shake and gyrate, the more pleasure men receive. This is not new. Indeed, if liberation were as simple as disrobing, exposing yourself in public, and having public sex, women would have been free long ago.

Moreover, as clearly outlined above, crimes against women, especially rape, have increased in Jamaica as has the incidence of domestic violence. In the face of this data, it is difficult to see how women have become empowered. I am not suggesting that dance hall is the cause of this increase. I am unequivocally asserting that sexual exhibitionism plays an important role in reifying the notion that women are sexual objects for the taking. Moreover, sexual freedom in the dance hall has not brought other freedoms to women at economic and political levels.

It appears that women who support dance hall behaviors are caught up in post-modernist mysticism—a world where anything goes. There is no real truth, indeed, no reality at all, and everyone's story is text—all of which have equal validity. Everything is "empowering" just because it exists. If there is a text that someone can create, then the creation itself, they would suggest, is empowering. Alas, in the dance hall, here is yet another case where "women hold power where there is no power to be held" (Douglass 1992). I suggest that spending time outside of the ivory tower and the dance hall and simply looking at the condition of Jamaicans in general, and women in particular, would indicate that "empowerment" is a figment of the imagination.

Even a cursory look into Jamaican society would reveal one sector in the dance hall attempting to display as much of their bodies as possible. Another sector is steeped in the Bible and spends discretionary time in prayer meetings. And yet another is busy reaffirming its superiority based on light skin color. While these groups are not mutually exclusive, members of this latter class, as well as foreign interlopers, are becoming increasingly comfortable as they consolidate their control over land and other resources that give them real power. It would be a sad case, indeed, if after centuries of suppression by this very class, women and other marginalized groups were obligated to "empower" themselves through public sex and exhibitionism.

Cross-Cultural Sexism in the African Diaspora

Jamaican reggae is not alone in its defamation of women through music. Negative depictions of women are rampant in African American music, most notably in rap and hip hop. Reggae and rap music, while sharing a common tendency towards negative attitudes and behaviors towards women, also share other characteristics. Like reggae, rap has been seen as a revolutionary force because it describes the "realities" of poor, urban populations.

But rap is not a monolithic musical form. As William Perkins points out, there are different waves of rap music (i.e. old school versus new school based on rap's historical development) and different types of rap music: gangsta rap, political or message rap, and "booty rap and retromack" (Perkins 1996:24). While each style has a particularly distinguishable character, all three types share trends towards misogyny.

Gangsta rap, popularized by such rappers and rap groups like the now defunct NWA, Ice-T, Dr. Dre and the Geto Boys, originated out of gang life in California. Known for its bleak portrayal of violence and street life, it is infamous in its treatment of women who are referred to as bitches and whores (hoes), as in one of Dr. Dre's songs entitled "Bitches ain't shit". The lyrics state, "Bitches ain't shit but hoes and tricks, lick on these nuts and suck my dick." Rap artist Ice-T defended this behavior in a radio interview: "That's how we are...that's how we talk in the ghetto...it's a black thang."

While many defend such usage as colloquial and harmless, I am still at a loss to understand how any African American can condone this derogatory language since I am certain that they do not think of their mothers as bitches or whores. (At least, I would like to be certain of this). It is not only the lyrics that show this connection between a portrayal of "blackness" and sexist attitudes towards women. Rap videos are also replete with scantily clad women who are often in compromising sexual positions.

In one of Dr. Dre's more popular videos, "Nuthin' but a G thang", featuring his protegé Snoop Doggy Dogg, a young woman who refuses the advances of a man in a crowded party is doused and drenched in Malt liquor in punishment for being a "bitch." It is clear from the perspective of the video that she has gotten what she deserved. There is no reference to the fact that any woman has the right to choose with whom she would or would not like to be with. In many ways she challenged what some males feel is their right to unlimited access and had to be "put in her place." The lyrics, while promoting safe sex and the use of contraceptives, refer to sex as "diggin' a bitch" and women are referred to as "hookas and hoes". This attitude towards women has not gone unnoticed by many African American women's groups who have protested against the obscenity and violence. In spite of these dissenting voices, unfortunately a wide enough audience exists that allows rappers to prosper.

Political or message rap falls into three categories: African centered, neo-nationalist, and Islamic (Perkins 1996:20). Groups like XCLAN, Public Enemy, and Brand Nubian fall respectively into these categories. Chuck D, the leader of Public Enemy and perhaps the foremost intellectual of political rap, uses not only lyrics but video to convey his revolutionary and often controversial messages. In the Public Enemy video "By the Time I get to Arizona" the fictional assassinations of the politicians who refused to make Martin Luther King Jr.'s birthday a state holiday are carried out by armed guerrillas. However, groups that see themselves as revolutionary are often the purveyors of anti-female self-determination. For example, Lord Jamar, a member of Brand Nubian (members of the Five Percent Nation), a group that separated from the Nation of Islam, feels that women should only be treated with respect if they live according to their "nature". Jamar states that

> If you really want to be with brothers like us...who have knowledge of themselves, then you have to have knowledge of yourselves too....or else you gotta be outa here, you know what I'm sayin'. [O]ur music rewards women who do right, who live according to their nature. If you're not living according to your nature..you could get dissed...basically (Gopaul 1994).

Since the Five Percent Nation's views on women do not differ from those of the Nation of Islam, women living according to their nature means being physically and ideologically shrouded.

Perhaps no other variety of rap music has caused a more general outcry of public censure than "booty rap and retro mack." 2 Live Crew is one group that exemplifies this particular vein. Their album "As Nasty as They Want to Be" was banned in parts of Florida for having "87 descriptions of oral sex, 116 mentions of male and female genitalia, and other lyrical passages referring to male ejaculation" (LeMoyne 1990). The lyrics were only matched by the group's antics on stage. Village Voice columnist Lisa Jones rebuts Henry Louis Gates Jr.'s defense of the group when she states, "I wonder if he's seen 2 Live Crew in concert, as I have, and watch them push women to the floor, pour water on them and chant, "Summer's Eve, Massengil, bitch wash your stinky pussy" (1990:171). This violence and degradation of women is a widespread phenomenon in rap music and in certain rappers' lives.

Women rap artists have taken two approaches in their own music. Some women like Sister Souljah and Queen Latifah have expressed positive ideas about the integrity of African American women. Other rappers have attempted to beat male rappers at their own game, with limited success. Rappers and groups like TLC and Salt-N-Pepa distinctly place men in the role of sexual objects, there for a woman's pleasure. Salt-N-Pepa's video "Shoop" begins with Salt, Pepa, and Spinderella at Coney Island watching the men who walk across the beach. The female gaze, as depicted in the video, is the male gaze in reverse. The women are directing their lyrics not at the men as a whole, but on specific body parts that pique their interest. The lyrics state,

> Can I get some fries
> with that shake, shake booty,

If looks could kill you might be an uzi or a shotgun,
Damn, what's up with that thang,
I want to know how does it hang.

While this is clearly a break from male-oriented sexual expression, the impact on its male viewers is questionable because the lyrics do not reflect the actual male-female dynamic which exists in society. Men are, indeed, being shown as studs, but in real life men do not think of men only as sexual objects so the lyrics have no meaning within our existing framework. Thus, these women rappers come off as simply horny or over-sexed. When men objectify women, on the other hand, the impact is immeasurably greater due to the fact that the lyrics are simply re-enforcing sex-roles established by a myriad of other language, behavioral and cultural patterns.

In the broad scheme of things, whether rap or reggae is degrading to women or denigrating the capitalist system, these popular media detract from any concerted, organized movement toward liberation. Liberation is a function of organization, sacrifice, and a willingness to do battle. For these things to happen, first and foremost, people must be willing to adopt new values.

Despite all the changes and developments in rap music in the past decade, one thing is absolutely clear — it is an extremely popular and profitable business that has more to do with selling records than inciting revolution. Undeniably, the very same system that some rappers attack, directly or indirectly, is the system that promotes rap music. Capitalist interests shape the image and output of many artists.

> While producers, music companies and rap artists become richer, people of African descent in this country struggle in their day to day lives to survive. It is also clear that rap music has had a long history of negative attitudes and behaviors towards women, and that is a legacy that has no foreseeable end, barring a total transformation in economic and social relations (Quiñones-Perdomo 1997).

Even though "conscious" rap is considered by many to be anti-establishment, artists applaud the materialist values that characterize capitalism by encouraging the purchase of Nautica, Tommy Hilfiger, and other elite brand names. When the song is over, most rap enthusiasts do not "Fight the Power," but spend precious time and money keeping up with the latest fashions. Similarly, roots reggae exhorts its followers to "Unite for the Africans abroad, unite for the Africans a yard, Africa, Unite... 'Cause we're moving right out of Babylon and we're going to our father's land" (Steel Pulse 1986).

These exhortations notwithstanding, there is no indication that Jamaicans who claim that such lyrics are revolutionary are becoming more conscious of their African heritage or struggling to free Jamaica from its U.S. satellite status. Instead, the penchant for a large sector of Jamaicans is to become as American as possible in manners, dress, speech, and spending patterns. The symbols of power are not a reflection of revolutionary work, but an enactment of media messages that glorify conspicuous consumption and, in the process, use women as commercial capital.

> [Jamaica] is theoretically empowered through the dissemination of its popular culture, yet is it the world which is extracting the "oil", reaping the economic benefits. This reinforces the idea, as articulated by Tomlinson, "that access to discourse is *always* linked to material—meaning, in a capitalist global order, economic—power" (Tomlinson [1991:]16). What is being implemented by the record industry is an incorporative rather than exclusionary racism (Gilroy, [1991:153], all the more lethal because it creates illusions of power which more easily defuse revolutionary potential (Alleyne 1994:82).

Even in the so-called "conscious" rap or reggae, women's power lies only in how women can serve men physically. Thus, while some lyrics speak to social injustice, on the whole, these genres remain androcentric and degrading to women. If we consider that both women and the European American power structures are being attacked, then how does that define the enemy?

Chapter 9

What's at Stake?

The Diffusion and Defusion of RastafarI

From the 1930s through the 1950s, Rastas represented an African Jamaican force that was invested in liberation from European capitalist hegemony. While it is true that from the beginning Rastas were andro-centric, at the same time, they were also more clear than Rastas are today about the necessity of self-government and the need to replace foreign and local elites. The days of Leonard Howell and Claudius Henry were ones where people were willing to wage war for their self-integrity as African people. Currently, Rasta appears to be synonymous with reggae and reefer.

In spite of a Rastafarian tendency to dissipate into the interstices of global culture, many scholars have referred to them as a revolutionary group. If this is so, then revolution has turned into an amalgam of symbols that appease Europeans by some mixture of "imperialist nostalgia"[1] (Ros-aldo 1989:68) and a superficial desire to identify with things African. Rasta seems to carry a similar mystique for a large sector of African and Dias-pora African people who defend Rasta and reggae with more passion than they repudiate the material and cultural genocide being waged against them.

Although many Jamaicans eschewed RastafarI and all that it stood for in the early days of the organization, acceptance of the group's symbols became widespread in the 1960s. After the University of the West Indies study (Smith et al. 1960) legitimated Rasta in the minds of many, it was mostly Jamaican youth who found within it a source of rebellion and iden-tity. A segment of the non-Rasta community also adopted Rasta dread-locks and Garveyite colors. Currently, red, black, green, and yellow are seen in all segments of Jamaican and Caribbean society. While some might interpret this as a sign of Rastafarian influence, it might also be interpret-ed as a diminution of the original intent of these symbols.

These colors, with the exception of yellow, are a legacy of Garvey's movement and have deep meaning for millions of continental and Dias-pora Africans around the world. Any effort to sum their significance is

---

1. Rosaldo describes a pretense on the part of many people of European descent to embrace all aspects of oppressed cultures in an attempt to undo or compensate for the past denigration of these same cultures.

difficult at best since the sum is greater than its parts. Nevertheless, it is safe to say that red, black, and green represent African people and their struggles for self-determination. As such, these symbols signified a movement for the people, of the people, and by the people.

Somewhere along the line, in the ranks of RastafarI, Garvey's goals got lost. They were lost, in part, by a willingness to allow Europeans into the organization. While some Rastas will allow anyone in who is willing to "sight Rasta," others have expressed difficulty with this policy. Indeed, it is difficult for some Rastas to understand what meaning "red" (the blood Diaspora Africans have shed in the struggle for emancipation) would have for European people. It is also unclear how "black," the symbol for African people, relates to European "Rastas?" Europeans who continue to oppress Africans and continue to wield white skin privilege now want to embrace what it means to be African. Finally, what meaning would "green," the symbol of the mother Africa, have for those not of African descent? To many African-descended people, it symbolizes our motherland — and mother has yet to adequately feed all of her children given the time she must spend feeding and fattening the European world.

There are individuals who will not allow Europeans into their fold. One Rastafarian woman contended that Europeans interested in the ideology of liberation should "go and form their own groups, but should not come in among Rastas." The only group that is adamant in this position are the Nyabingi. Some others accept people of European descent based on the proposal that "all those who open their hearts to Jah are welcome."

Accompanying this open door policy, Jamaican elites and foreign entrepreneurs have appropriated Rastafarian symbols for the monetary return they offer. Commercial establishments utilize Rasta colors and co-opt linguistic expressions in order to capitalize on the tourist dollar. Rasta imagery such as Bob Marley and expressions like "Irie Mon" emblazoned on T-shirts and other paraphernalia have come to represent Rasta in the minds of a large sector of the local and foreign public. Thus, once again, elites exploit African culture for their own advantage, and, in the process, degrade Rastas with such symbols as "Dread Dog," a picture of a mean looking bull-dog with dreadlocks and blood shot eyes.

Many Rastafarian men have contributed to this commercialization through their own activities with European and European American tourists. Rasta men regularly proposition women. Even though these advances are made to women of African and European descent, from all appearances, it is women of European descent who come to Jamaica with the primary purpose of finding a Rasta man. So common is this practice in Jamaica that it has become known as "rent-a-Rasta." The tourist beaches and perennial reggae extravaganza are venues where these activities abound. I am not suggesting that the majority of Rasta men engage in these endeavors, but that they are common enough to influence the image of Rasta as well as the cohesiveness of the organization. All of this is quite unfortunate since Rastafarians had the potential of leading the most progressive movement of African people since Marcus Garvey. This potential has been thwarted by a number of historical misinterpretations and cultural practices that render true liberation improbable.

Given the physical and ideological dissipation of RastafarI, one Rasta woman I spoke with wondered about its chances for survival. She said that she was afraid that in the near future, "if Rastas do not begin to organize around concrete issues, it might not be uncommon to hear people say 'once upon a time there was a group of people called Rasta'" (Lake 1993). It is my sense that Rasta will be around for a long time. What they will come to stand for is a different story.

One of the biggest problems is that Rastas have resigned themselves to a very ahistorical view of Africa. Ironically, their acceptance of their African identity is the key to their ability to influence and mobilize other people of African descent; however, they have missed this opportunity given that they ignore the very hierarchical nature of ancient and present African social systems.

A case in point is their veneration of Haile Selassie as god or as an important leader since Selassie was one of the most demagogic African leaders in the twentieth century whose centralization of power resulted in the marginalization of many Ethiopians. In conversations with Rastas, one soon learns that attempts to raise these issues leads nowhere. Their unrealistic view of Selassie's power is indicated by the contention that, given his divine status, he is still alive. Many people view Rastafarians with skepticism because of this mystification. As stated by Leachim Semaj (a former Rastafarian),

> [t]his represents a serious problem in our development because any attempt to falsify the facts regarding the past or the present inevitably makes the prospects for understanding the future very bleak, and many times impossible. One may be able to fool one's self and feel good but the material reality will remain the same (1985:25).

Religious Obstacles

The fact that Rasta is steeped in religious ideology is problematic since religion has always represented a way of legitimating hierarchical relations in material society. Religion has served as a fifth column for men the world over who seek not only to dominate women, but to convince them that their suppression is "God's will." Moreover, religion has been used by people of African descent as a means to escape from the realistic material conditions and from a sense of hopelessness. If we cannot find the solution in this world, we will find it in the afterlife. Religious mythology, or any mythology, can only be useful in the quest for liberation if it advances the cause for all people, not just a segment who wishes to acquire or retain its dominant position.

Since religion has never accomplished this, perhaps it needs to be replaced with a philosophy created by women and men and one that speaks to the total transformation of social relationships. If Rasta is truly about development, in the pure sense of the word, then the obvious question is how can they perceive the process of development taking place with only half of its population?

Men Resist Women's Initiatives

Why has so much energy been used to codify 'woman as subordinate' in cultural and political institutions? What is at stake? I suggest that what is at stake is male power. Whether power is demonstrated by control over the means of production, control over cultural institutions or religious texts, men think they have a lot to lose. Power is also experienced in the household where women defer to men and/or where women are victims of male violence. It seems that men who perpetrate violence against women and those who work against the general liberation of women are not interested in true democracy, but a pseudo-democracy where men remain in control.

In a wonderful film that depicts the relative status of Rastafarian women, *RastafarI: Conversations Concerning Woman* (Lieb and Romano 1983), the narrator speaks of resistance to any conversation about the position of women within the movement. Any attempts to break the silence is met with accusations of being too "western," "disloyal," or "lesbian." I find these responses interesting if only for their commonality around the world. Not only are these common male responses to any attempt by women to liberate themselves (or even talk about the possibility), but women also buy into these criticisms.

At the same time, there has been a small sector of Rastafarian women who have been trying to bring about change. In the 1980s these women initiated three organizations that were intended to address the educational needs of Rasta children, social services within the Rastafarian community, and other forms of self-development. The groups formed were The International Twelve (Twelve Tribes); King Alpha and Queen Omega's Theocracy Daughters, a group of elder Rasta sisters from Theocracy; and Dawtas United (DAWTAS).

In a conversation with Maureen Rowe in 1997 she explained the purpose of Dawtas United and the reasons for its demise.

> We wanted to achieve something—to feed the hungry and clothe the poor. We started off with a lot of enthusiasm, but part of the problem was that some of the sisters wanted to spend more time chanting than planning agendas. [Moreover], there was a lot of resistance from the males. Sisters started to drift because their kingmen gave them a hard time for going to meetings. Some accused their women of being lesbians and being part of the group so they could talk about men.

After a while the men became paranoid to the point of coming to the meetings which they and some of the women thought gave it more legitimacy. Other sisters began to ask why it was that their meetings needed to be validated by having men present.

This, and personal dissension among the sisters, eventually led to the demise of this and other women's organizations. Financial capital was another problem. DAWTAS had planned to set up a school for children. They organized a number of fund raising activities, but found that they could not raise sufficient capital to meet the necessary expenses. Even though the problems that DAWTAS faced were multifaceted, many of them came from direct or indirect male influence. This reaction on the part of Rasta males is not different from that in other women's organizations.

We see the effective use of these silencing mechanisms in the Chicana movement in the United States where women are led to believe that if they speak about male dominance within their own communities, then they are hurting the larger Chicano cause. Such "troublemakers" are often labelled *vendidas* (sell-outs) or lesbians (Garcia 1989:226–227). Because many women think that being a lesbian is the worst thing in the world, this label is effectively used by men to prevent women from advocating on their own behalf. The accusation is more than ironic since men who level such accusations are implying that heterosexual women would not possibly seek greater freedoms because they are happy with their present condition. Therefore, anyone who speaks about women's liberation must be a lesbian. Since women have also been taught from the day they were born to be silent and to allow men to take the lead, these strategies are effective "red herrings."

Likewise, in the African American community in the United States there is this long-standing volatile debate as to whether women should concentrate on issues of male dominance within their own communities (some say this dominance does not exist), or put all of their energies into the struggle for African American equality. This situation is mind boggling since the fight for equality as women or as African descended people is not mutually exclusive. Nevertheless, the logic goes something like this: We (as African people, qua African male people) need to achieve our freedom first, and then we'll work on the women's problems! What is even more astounding than this oft repeated scenario is that both men and women espouse this illogical rhetoric. It is difficult to imagine how anyone can form their mouths to utter such statements since they suggest that one group's oppression is more important than another's. But these priorities remain extant since women are conditioned from the day they are born to assume a back seat. Women of African descent in all areas of the Diaspora have been taught that the struggle for liberation means "Black" *male* power.

In the Caribbean, during the slave period and in the postbellum era

> the male slave was not only in an economically superior position compared with the female, but played virtually all religious, political and economic leadership roles in slave society;... female subordination was the norm then, and continues to be a feature of Caribbean society ever since (Senior 1991:95 following Mathurin 1975).

Since the time of slavery, liberation has been couched in male terms. During African American repatriation movements, leaders such as Henry McNeal Turner repeatedly opined that black *men* would never experience true equality in America. In the 1950s and 1960s African American participants in the civil rights movement lobbied to gain access to public accommodations, voting rights for all African Americans, and higher wages. Some of these demonstrations were accompanied by men wearing signs which read, "*I am a man.*" Was this the point of the civil rights movement? Or was it that we are all equal human beings and, therefore, deserve equal treatment and equal access?

A Rastafarian woman speaks eloquently about this kind of bigotry that perpetuates the marginalization of oppressed groups and denounces solidarity among women.

> We cannot replace bigotry with bigotry. We have a higher calling than that. African people and people of color have a higher calling than to replace with a black or colored skin a lot of the nastiness and injustice that exists with human beings in the world now. And we cannot do that if we do not recognize that injustice feeds upon another side of the coin of the bigotry that is practiced against homosexuals, that's practiced against workers, that's practiced against disabled people, that's practiced against women, that's practiced against children, then we have not gone anywhere. When you have sexuality hysteria, bigotry, it even serves to set back this movement because sisters feel funny about expressing love toward each other for fear that they might be branded as that [homosexual]. In the process of our march for freedom, we're going to have to free all of humanity (Lake 1993).

These ideals are sound, but will be a long time coming in a society where everyday practices privilege males. At very young ages boys and girls are sex-typed through the clothes they wear, the games they are allowed to play, and the way they spend their time and energy. Household chores, which begin when the child is around five years old are among the most important arenas where sex differentiation occurs and where girls are more often relegated to the domestic sphere (Cohen 1955; Justus 1981). Women are also taught to be subservient to men and to defer to them in domestic and public matters (Senior 1991, Douglass 1992).

A clear example of this deference is depicted in a child character in George Lamming's novel, *In the Castle of My Skin*

> Third boy: Rat's father...support[s] all of them good good good, an' they don't want for anything in this God's world. But they ain't got no freedom. When he ain't there the house is like a concert, "cause the mother is a sweet woman who gives plenty jokes, but as soon as he put in his appearance, everybody stop talking. 'Tis funny the way it happens. You hear the talking talking talking, an' suddenly somebody say easy easy, daddy comin', an' suddenly everything is like a black-out for the ears. You don't hear anything at all. Not a sound but their father foot out coming through the yard. An' it stay silent so till he go out again (Lamming 1970:44–45).

Even though this is a fictional account, it accurately represents the role of the father or adult male as head of the household. Uneven relations at the familial level are part of a broader political-economic and cultural environment where male power and privilege over females is the order of the day. During my field research I observed these same dynamics within Rastafarian families. While talking to women in their homes, when a man entered the room, he would become the spokesperson for both of them. Fortunately, not all Rastafarian women could be silenced by men in this way.

> I'd say that Rasta women are in the forefront in terms of African-Jamaican women and are the Jamaican women who really stand up in livity in the society and who have to be respected. It is my honest view that Rasta women need more support from Rasta men, more real support.... Sometimes the initiative and spirit of the Rasta woman is many times too oppressed.... And I think this type of attitude, this behavior, keeps back both the Rasta man and the Rasta woman. Because I think that it is the woman, in the same way that I said that Black people have a special responsibility in fighting for our freedom and for freedom for all peoples — similarly women as a gender have that responsibility. They should clear the roadblocks which men put up in front of them.

There were other women who clearly saw themselves in control of their own lives. Invariably these were women who were not dependent on men, economically or otherwise. One woman was forceful in expressing the source of her independence.

> It's Rasta women that's holdin' the money now and we refuse to be treated like footstools because it's not working.

> Initially the Rasta woman played a passive bit in the Rasta community —
> very much in the background. She would keep the family together. She
> was very much behind her kingman. Her major role was maintaining the
> family structure, the bearer of children and so on. What has happened over
> the years is that the nature of our society and the growth of the Rastafar-
> ian movement in general has caused the woman to become more outgoing.

The fact that most of the women who held more progressive views were
also more economically independent was not coincidental. Rastafarian
women, as well as women everywhere, tend to embrace their own subordination for two primary reasons: first, they are beholden to men because
of the financial support men sometimes offer (in the case of Jamaicans this
economic support is often meager). Secondly, female children are taught at
very young ages that their place in society is less valued than that of their
male counterparts. These factors are mutually reinforcing.

Any study of RastafarI is important not because Rastas are so distinct,
but because they reflect the sexist behaviors in Jamaica (and the African
Diaspora) as a whole. Indeed any treatise on Rasta, given their numbers,
would be insignificant if this were not the case. Rastafari beliefs regarding
women constitute a microcosmic and exaggerated version of Jamaican
views of, and treatment of, women as a whole.

Just as men dominate Rastafarian nyabingis and religious services, so
it is with other non-Rastafarian religious groups. There are women ministers, but they are the exception rather than the rule. In society at large,
men who live in households with women are considered the heads of households whether they are making more money than women or not. Rastas
share the same belief. Non-Rastas may not explicitly state that women are
polluted because of their capacity to menstruate, but based on empirical
research (Chevannes n.d.), most men do not have sexual relationships with
women during their menstruation. Other behaviors suggest the similarity
between Rastas and non-Rastas.

Jamaican women do not wear the geles (head wraps) that many Rasta
women use to cover their hair, but during religious gatherings in conven-
tional churches, women are expected to cover their hair, not men. So while
Rastas distinguish themselves in many of their beliefs and practices, there
are other ways in which the subordination of Rastafarian and non-Rastafarian females is coterminous. These proscriptions operate to place limits
on women's mobility and to validate the idea of their inferiority.

The Effectiveness of Women's Organizations

There are a myriad of Jamaican women's organization that have proliferated in the past ten years in response to women's economic inferiori-

ty and violence against women. Some of these organizations have made important practical differences in women's lives; others have tried to create theoretical bases that would rectify the status of women. In the short run, some of these efforts are sorely needed, e.g, female police officers in rape units who counsel and support rape victims. Rape crisis centers are also important in giving women legal and emotional support. In the area of job training, the Women's Construction Collective, formed in 1983, has been instrumental in teaching women non-traditional skills that can widen their employment opportunities. In spite of these and other measures which have ameliorated women's circumstances to a degree, larger problems persist. These problems emanate from the fact that these organizations do not attack the root of the problem—male institutional control.

This control is situated within a capitalist society which, by definition, thrives off of and exists by virtue of an unemployed and underemployed constituency. As is discussed in Chapter Five, women make up the majority of these people. In addition to being superexploited over and above men, women are sexually exploited on the job as well as in their private lives. What exacerbates the problem is that women's own behaviors, which they have learned from childhood, demonstrate a deference to men in almost all things, a catering to men, and very rigid ideas as to their own comportment.

In order to dismantle this male controlled system, it is necessary to understand that power is never relinquished willingly. Jamaican women must form coalitions with other people of African descent who are committed to true freedom. Such alliances must be preceded by the understanding that wresting power from European and other males only to be replaced by African varieties, will not bring about liberation. Liberation must be for women, children, and men and must be tantamount to direct control over valuable resources that will be equally shared. This should not be a radical idea, but, alas, it is.

The question of capitalism is not addressed in many women's organizations. Up to this point, they have assumed the existence of capitalism and have worked to train women to work within this milieu. As mentioned above, there are some skills, such as construction work, that will be useful in a liberated territory; however, the majority of training offered to women has been in traditionally female oriented skills such as sewing, cooking, and needlecraft. Even in these areas, women are, more often than not, unable to find jobs that will afford them a viable income (AWOJA Report, n.d.:7).

At the theoretical level, these mistakes are repeated. Many academics contribute to the problem of women's subordination by bandying around terms like "gender, race, and class," "patriarchy," and "empowerment." The harm is not in the terms themselves but in the fact that these words are used repeatedly as if they themselves will extricate women from the powers that bind them. What, in fact, happens is that the authors of these words create a profusion of literature on "patriarchy" that advances their own careers, but makes little progress for the masses of women. As for my own work on Rasta and other women's containment, I have done nothing if readers do not begin to understand that writing and reading are not enough. We must take action to liberate ourselves from male control. Whatever means we use — and we must use any means necessary — it must be of our own making and it must seek to totally dismantle all forms of hierarchy. At the level of culture, one Rasta women put it most clearly when she said that the end to male hegemony would require

> women being clearer in their minds, having plans for their lives. Looking forward more confident. Women not requiring to have a medium between them and their God, talking to God directly. We don't need nobody to talk to God for us because God listens to everybody who call upon him — he, she or it. So I mean to say that women need to take our destiny on our hands.
>
> We have to take the responsibility for that because there were many slaves who never wanted slavery to end. There were two suits of clothes, whether it's calico or whatever, from the slave master. You get at least one meal a day, your little plot so you can hustle and sell things in the eternal market. And there were too many slaves who didn't want to fight because this was a more comfortable and an easy way out. And if it meant supping everything that the slave master gave, friending up with the slave master, leaving yourself at the will of the slave master, then they did it. There were too many of us, and are still many of us who are still willing to do that. Because on the other road, you have to work out how to get your food yourself, how you're going to get your clothes yourself. But what a tremendous freedom. It's more difficult, but what a tremendous freedom. What glory. And similarly, the Rasta woman is going to have to find a path which links her with all of her sisters in genuine sisterhood and relates more to the brothers as brothers and co-travellers and not the dominated and the dominator.

Appendices

Appendix A

Rastafarian Chronology

1887   Marcus Mosiah Garvey born in St. Ann's Bay, Jamaica.

1914   Garvey organized the Universal Negro Improvement and Conservation Association and African Communities League in Kingston, Jamaica.

1917   Garvey organizes first branch of the Universal Negro Improvement Association (UNIA) in New York City.

1919   Garvey incorporates steamship company, the Black Star Line, in the state of Delaware.

1919   Garvey marries Amy Ashwood at Liberty Hall, New York City.

1922   Garvey is arrested along with other Black Star Line officials for allegedly using the mail to defraud.

1922   Garvey marries Amy Jacques in Baltimore, Maryland.

1927   President Coolidge commutes Garvey's sentence and deports him to Jamaica.

1929   Sixth International Convention of the United Negro Improvement Association in Kingston, Jamaica.

1930   Coronation of Ras Tafari as Emperor Haile Selassie.

1932   The Ethiopian Coptic Faith is instituted in Jamaica.

1934   Leonard Howell arrested for using seditious language. Sentenced to two years in prison.

1935   Marcus Garvey fails to resuscitate UNIA in Jamaica and returns to England.

1935   Leonard Howell arrested by British authorities in Jamaica for delivering what was called a "seditious speech."

1935   Claudius Henry arrested for preaching without a license.

1937   Haile Selassie sends his cousin, Dr. Malaku E. Bayen, to New York to establish the Ethiopian World Federation. On August 25, 1937 the Ethiopian World Federation (EWF) comes into being.

1938   Working class revolt that results in important labor reforms.

1938   The first EWF office in Jamaica was Local 17.

1940   Leonard Howell forms Ethiopian Salvation Society at Pinnacle.

1941   The Pinnacle is raided by police and Howell, along with twenty eight other members, is arrested. They were charged with violence and growing marijuana.

1941   Howell is released and returns to Pinnacle.

1954   Police raid closes down Pinnacle. Howell arrested but later acquitted.

1955   Haile Selassie grants 500 acres of land to "Black people of the West" in return for their support during the Italian invasion of Ethiopia. This land was administered through the Ethiopian World Federation.

1955   Mami Richardson, a leading EWF official, visits Jamaica and is instrumental in establishing local EWF branches island wide.

1958   Prince Edward calls Rastafarians to Kingston Pen adjoining Back O' Wall to launch repatriation to Africa. Repatriation did not transpire.

1958   Bobo Shanti community is burned down by police.

1959   Rev. Claudius Henry establishes the Seventh Emmanuel Brethren and the African Reform Church.

1959   Claudius arrested for selling false tickets for passage back to Africa.

1960   Howell detained at Kingston Mental Asylum. Arms cache discovered with Rasta leader.

1960   Claudius Henry and nine of his followers arrested for seditious activities. Ammunition and an arms cache were seized at Henry's headquarters.

1960   Government initiates full investigation of RastafarI. Study carried out by University of West Indies faculty and a small group of Rastafarians.

1961   Government sends Rastafarian mission to Africa.
(April) Mission returns on 2 June 1961.

1962   Jamaica gains independence from England.

1963   Campaign to eliminate *ganja*.

1964   Garvey's remains are exhumed in England and reinterred in the Marcus Garvey Mausoleum in National Heroes Park in Kingston, Jamaica.

1966   Haile Selassie visits Jamaica.

1968   Walter Rodney barred from reentering Jamaica.

1980   Walter Rodney assassinated in Guyana.

1980   Rastafarian women form three groups: King Alpha and Queen Omega's Theocracy Daughters, International Twelve, and Dawtas United (DAWTAS).

1980   50th Anniversary of the Coronation of Haile Selassie.

1981   Bob Marley dies in Miami, Florida.

1993   Haile Selassie centennial celebrated in Jamaica.

1997   (August 1) Emancipation Day, organized by Minion Phillips (Sister Minnie), was commemorated for the first time.

1997   (August 3) Jamaican independence day held the first Monday in August.

Appendix B

Summary of Recommendations

University of the West Indies Committee Report

1. The Government of Jamaica should send a mission to African countries to arrange for immigration of Jamaicans. Representatives of Ras Tafari brethren should be included in the mission.
2. Preparations for the mission should be discussed immediately with representatives of the Ras Tafari brethren.
3. The general public should recognize that the great majority [of] Ras Tafari brethren are peaceful citizens, willing to do an honest day's work.
4. The police should complete their security enquiries rapidly, and cease to persecute peaceful Ras Tafari brethren.
5. The building of low-rent houses should be accelerated, and provisions made for self-help cooperative building.
6. Government should acquire the principal areas where squatting is now taking place, and arrange for water, light, sewerage disposal and collection of rubbish.
7. Civic centers should be built with facilities for technical classes, youth clubs, child clinics, etc. The churches and the U.C.W.I. should collaborate.
8. The Ethiopian Orthodox Coptic Church should be invited to establish a branch in West Kingston.
9. Ras Tafari brethren should be assisted to establish cooperative workshops.
10. Press and radio facilities should be accorded to leading members of the movement.

Smith, et al. 1960:38.

Appendix C

Numbers of Rastafarians by Parish—1982 Census

	Male Rastas 0–44 yrs. old	Female Rastas 0–44 yrs.old	Females Over 45 yrs. old
All Jamaica	10,574	2,422	166
Kingston	644	106	6
St. Andrew	2,850	920	53
St. Thomas	632	132	7
Portland	339	48	1
St. Mary	494	88	6
St. Ann	558	61	6
Trelawny	371	38	6
St. James	605	149	14
Hanover	316	43	3
Westmorland	608	106	4
St. Elizabeth	495	65	5
Manchester	460	89	3
Clarendon	769	195	23
St.Catherine	1,433	382	29

Compiled from *Population Census*, 1982

Appendix D

Religious Affiliation in Jamaica

Church of God	400,379
Anglican	154,548
Seventh Day Adventist	150,722
Roman Catholic	95,712
Moravian Church	25,000
Methodist	18,284
United Church of Jamaica	13,450
National Spiritual Assembly	6,300
Islam	2,238
United Congregation of Israelites	250

The Europa World Yearbook (1995:164-1665)

Appendix E

Twelve Tribes of Israel

Twelve Tribes	Hebrew Months	Julian Months
Reuben	Nisan (Abib)	March-April
Simeon	Iyyar (Ziv)	April-May
Levi	Sivan	May-June
Judah	Tammuz	June-July
Issachar	Ab	July-August
Zebulun	Elul	August-September
Dan	Tishri (Ethanim)	September-October
Asher	Chislev	November-December
Naphtali	Tebeth	December-January
Joseph	Shebat	January-February
Benjamin	Adar	February-March

Bibliography

Abu-Lughod, Lila
1986 *Veiled Sentiments. Honor and Poetry in a Bedouin Society.*
Berkeley: University of California Press.

Abeng
1969 Interview with Marcus Garvey, Jr. (June 14).

_____
1969 Women. (March 1) 1:2.

Achebe, Chinua
1976 *Things Fall Apart.* London: Heinemann.

Ahmed, Leila
1992 *Women and Gender in Islam: Historical Roots of a Modern Debate.* New Haven: Yale University Press.

Alexander, Jacqui M.
1994 Not Just (Any) *Body* Can Be a Citizen: The Politics of Law, Sexuality and Post-Coloniality in Trinidad and Tobago and the Bahamas. *Feminist Review.* 48:5–23

Alleyne, Mike
1994 Positive Vibration?: Capitalist Textual Hegemony and Bob Marley. *Bulletin of Eastern Caribbean Affairs.* 19(3):76–84.

Anderson, Beverly and Winston Langley
1988 Women as Depicted in Music in Jamaica. Caribbean Studies Association, XIV Annual Conference, Barbados.

Anderson, Patricia
1987 Informal Sector or Secondary Labour Market? Towards a Synthesis. *Social and Economic Studies.* 36(3):149–176.

Antrobus, Peggy and Lorna Gordon
1984 The English-Speaking Caribbean: A Journey in the Making. In *Sisterhood is Global. The International Women's Movement Anthology,* pp.118–126. Robin Morgan (Ed.). Garden City: Anchor Books/Doubleday.

Antrobus, Peggy (Ed.)
1987 Gender Implications of the Debt Crisis. In *Development in Suspense,* pp.145–160. Conference of Caribbean Economists. Kingston: Friedrich Ebert Stiftung.

Asante, S.K.
1977 *Pan-African Protest: West Africa and the Italo-Ethiopian Crisis, 1934–1941.* London: Longman Group Ltd.

Austin-Broos, Diane J.
1987 Pentacostals and Rastafarians: Cultural, Political, and Gender Relations of Two Religious Movements. *Social and Economic Studies.* 36(4):1–39.

AWOJA
n.d. *Moving Forward. The Work, Realities and Visions of Women's Organizations in Jamaica. 1985–1995.* Kingston, Jamaica: Balanced Graphics.

Bailey, Barbara
1987 Opportunities for Women in Non-Formal Education in Jamaica: The Case of HEART. Paper prepared for the first Interdisciplinary Seminar of Women and Development Studies. Gender, Culture and Caribbean Development.

Barrett, Leonard
1988 *The Rastafarians. Sounds of Cultural Dissonance.* Boston: Beacon Press.

———
1977 *The Rastafarians—Dreadlocks of Jamaica.* Kingston: Sangsters.

Bart, Pauline and Eileen Moran
1993 *Violence Against Women. The Bloody Footprints.* Sage Publications.

Becker, Mary
1994 Religion and Equality for Women. Paper presented at the Law and Society Meeting, June 1994, Phoenix, Arizona.

Beckford, George
1988 *Persistent Poverty. Underdevelopment in Plantation Economies of the Third World.* Morant Bay, Jamaica: Maroon Publishing House.

Beckford, George and Michael Witter
1980 *Small Garden…Bitter Weed.* London: Zed Press.

Beckles, Hilary
1995 Sex and Gender in the Historiography of Caribbean Slavery. In *Engendering History. Caribbean Women in Historical Perspective*, pp. 125–140. Verene Shepherd, Bridget Brereton, and Barbara Bailey (Eds.). New York: St. Martin's Press.

———
    1987 *Black Rebellion in Barbados. The Struggle against Slavery.*
    Bridgetown: Carib Research and Publication, Inc.
Beers, William
    1992 *Women and Sacrifice: Male Narcissism and the Psychology
    of Religion.* Detroit: Wayne State University Press.
Bible
    1989 1 Corinthians. *The Holy Bible.* Nashville: T. Nelson
    Publishers.

———
    1989 Deuteronomy. *The Holy Bible.* Nashville: T. Nelson
    Publishers.

———
    1989 Exodus 10:12. *The Holy Bible.* Nashville: T. Nelson
    Publishers.

———
    1989 Genesis. *The Holy Bible.* Nashville: T. Nelson Publishers.

———
    1989 Judges. *The Holy Bible.* Nashville: T. Nelson Publishers.

———
    1989 Leviticus. *The Holy Bible.* Nashville: T. Nelson Publishers.

———
    1989 Numbers. *The Holy Bible.* Nashville: T. Nelson Publishers.

———
    1989 Psalms. *The Holy Bible.* Nashville: T. Nelson Publishers.
Bilby, Kenneth
    1977 The Impact of Reggae in the United States. *Popular Music
    and Society.* 5:5.
Black, Clinton
    1965 *History of Jamaica.* London: Collins Clear-Type Press.
Bolles, Lynn
    1983 Kitchens Hit by Priorities: Employed Working-Class
    Jamaican Women Confront the IMF. In *Men, Women, and the
    International Division of Labor,* pp. 138–160. June Nash and
    Marcia Patricia Fernandez-Kelly (Eds.). Albany: State University
    of New York Press.

———
    1996 *Sister Jamaica. A Study of Women, Work and Households in
    Jamaica.* New York: University Press of America.

Boot, A. and V. Goldman
1981   *Soul Rebel—Natural Mystic*. London: Hutchinson.

Bopp, William J. and James J. Vardalis
1987   *Crimes Against Women*. Springfield: Charles C. Thomas.

Bosmajian, Haig
1992   The Language of Sexism. In *Race, Class, and Gender in the United States: An Integrated Study*, pp.341–347. Paula S. Rothenberg (Ed.). New York: St. Martin's Press.

Brain, J.
1978   Symbolic Rebirth: The Mwali Rite among the Luguru of Eastern Tanzania. *Africa*. 48(2):176–188.

Brathwaite, Kamau
1984   Caribbean Women during the Period of Slavery. Elsa Goveia Memorial Lecture, Cave Hill campus. Barbados.

_____
1971   *The Development of Creole Society in Jamaica*. Oxford: Clarendon Press.

Braude, Monique C., and Jacqueline P. Ludford
1984   Marijuana Effects on the Endocrine and Reproductive Systems. NIDA Research Monograph 44. Department of Health and Human Services. Rockville: National Institute on Drug Abuse.

Brodber, Erna
1986   Afro-Jamaican Women at the Turn of the Century. *Social and Economic Studies*. 35(3):23–50.

_____
1975   *Yards in the City of Kingston*. Mona: Institute of Social and Economic Research, University of the West Indies.

Brown, Barbara
1989   Women in Botswana. In *Women and Development in Africa. Comparative Perspectives*, pp. 257–278. Jane Parpart (Ed.). Lanham, Maryland: University Press of America, Inc.

Brown, Joanne
1994   Because of the Angels: Sexual Violence and Abuse. In *Violence against Women*, pp. 3–10. Elisabeth Schussler Fiorenza and M. Shawn Copeland. London: SCM Press.

Buckley, Thomas and Alma Gottleib
1988   *Blood Magic: The Anthropology of Menstruation*. Berkeley: University of California Press.

Burks, Mary Fair
1993 Trailblazers: Women in the Montgomery Bus Boycott. In
*Women in the Civil Rights Movement. Trailblazers and
Torchbearers, 1941–1965,* pp. 71–83. Vicki L. Crawford,
Jacqueline Anne Rouse, and Barbara Woods (Eds.). Bloomington:
Indiana University Press.
Bush, Barbara
1990 *Slave Women in Caribbean Society 1650–1830.*
Bloomington: Indiana University Press.
Campbell, Horace
1990 *Rasta and Resistance. From Marcus Garvey to Walter
Rodney.* Trenton: African World Press.

––––––
1980 Rastafari: Culture of Resistance. *Race and Class.*
22(1):1–22.

––––––
1985 The Rastafarians in the Eastern Caribbean. *Caribbean
Quarterly.* 25:42–61.
Campbell, Sadie
1974 Folklore and Food Habits. *Jamaica Journal.* 8(2–3):56–59.

––––––
1974 Bush Teas. A Cure-All. *Jamaica Journal.* 8(2–3):60–65.
Cashmore, Ernest E.
1979 *Rastaman: The Rastafarian Movement in England.* London:
Unwin Paperbacks.
Cathcart, Jenny
1989 *Hey You! A Portrait of Youssou N'Dour.* England: Fine Line
Books.
Chaney, Elsa M. and Martha W. Lewis
1985 *Women, Migration and the Decline of Smallholder
Agriculture.* Working Paper #97. University of the West Indies,
Mona Campus.
Chevannes, Barry (Ed.)
1995 *Rastafari and Other African-Caribbean Worldviews.*
London: Macmillan.

––––––
n.d. Don't Be a Gladys: The Sex Life of Jamaican Men. Research
Report. Kingston: University of the West Indies, Mona.

_____
1990 Healing the National: RastafarI Exorcism of the Ideology of Racism in Jamaica. *Caribbean Quarterly.* 36(1–2):59–84.

_____
1993 Sexual Behavior of Jamaicans. *Social and Economic Studies.* 42(1):1–45.

_____
1988 *Marijuana. Background to Drug Use in Jamaica,* pp. 7–19. Kingston: Institute of Social and Economic Research.
Clarke, Peter
1994 *Black Paradise. The Rastafarian Movement.* San Bernardino: Borgo Press.
Clarke, Sebastion
1980 *Jah Music: The Evolution of the Popular Jamaican Song.* London: Heinemann Educational Books Ltd.
Cohen, Yehudi
1955 Character Formation and Social Structure in a Jamaican Community. *Psychiatry: Journal for the Study of Interpersonal Processes.* (August) 18:3.
Collins, Patricia Hill
1990 *Black Feminist Thought: Knowledge, Consciousness and the Politics of Empowerment.* Boston: Unwin Hyman.
Collinwood, Dean and Osamu Kusatsu
n.d. *Japanese Rastafarians: Non-Conformity in Modern Japan.* Ann Arbor, Michigan: Institute for Social Research.
Cooper, Carolyn
1993 *Noises in the Blood: Orality, Gender and the "Vulgar" Body of Jamaican Popular Culture.* London: Macmillan.

_____
1994 Commentary in *The Darker Side of Black.* Videorecording. Lina Gopaul, Director.
Cronon, Edmund D.
1955 *Black Moses: The Story of Marcus Garvey and the Universal Negro Improvement Association.* Madison: The University of Wisconsin Press.
Curtin, Philip
1955 *Two Jamaicas.* Cambridge: Harvard University Press.

Cushman, Thomas
   1991 Rich Rastas and Communist Rockers: A Comparative Study
   of the Origin, Diffusion and Defusion of Revolutionary Musical
   Codes. *Journal of Popular Culture.* 25(3):17–61.
Daily Gleaner
   1993 Ganja Farming Increases. (June 20):1.
Daily Gleaner
   1960 Members of First Africa Corps Sons and Daughters of
   Africa. 66 in U.S. banned from Landing Here. (October 28):1.
Daily Gleaner
   1960 This Menace to Our Future. (October 19):10.
Daily Gleaner
   1960 October 5, 1959 Named Back-to-Africa Deadline. (October
   11):1, 5.
Daily Gleaner
   1960 Reports from Witnesses at Henry's Trial. (October 7).
Daily Observer
   1997 Emancipation, Reparation and Spanish Town. (August
   11):7.
Davies, Omar and Patricia Anderson
   1987 The Impact of the Recession and Adjustment Policies on
   Poor Urban Women in Jamaica. Paper prepared for UNICEF.
   Kingston: University of West Indies.
Davis, Stephen
   1990. *Bob Marley.* Vermont: Schenkman.
Davis, Stephen and Peter Simon
   1983 *Reggae International.* London: Thames and Hudson.
Deere, Carmen, Peggy Antrobus, Lynn Bolles, Edwin Melendez, Peter
   Phillips, Marcia Rivera, and Helen Safa
   1990 *In the Shadows of the Sun.* Boulder: Westview Press.
Donnell, Allison and Sarah Lawson Welsh
   1996 *The Routledge Reader in Caribbean Literature.* Routledge:
   London.
Douglas, Mary
   1970 *Natural Symbols: Explorations in Cosmology.* New York:
   Pantheon Books.

Douglass, Lisa
1992 *The Power of Sentiment. Love, Hierarchy and the Jamaican Family Elite.* Boulder: Westview Press.
Drucker, Peter
1996 "In the Tropics There is No Sin": Sexuality and Gay-Lesbian Movements in the Third World. *New Left Review.* 218:75–101.
Dunfee, Susan Nelson
1989 *Beyond Servanthood. Christianity and the Liberation of Women.* Lanham: University Press of America, Inc.
Du Toit, Brian M.
1980 *Cannabis in Africa*, pp. 11–18. Rotterdam: A.A. Balkema.
Eaton, George
1975 *Alexander Bustamente and Modern Jamaica.* Kingston: Kingston Publishers Limited.
The Economist
1994 Reggae Music. Trench Town East. (January 22):95.
Edwards, Bryan
1973 Observations on the Disposition, Character, Manners, and Habits of Life, of the Maroon Negroes of the Island of Jamaica; and a Detail of the Origin, Progress, and Termination of the War between those People and the White Inhabitants. In *Maroon Societies: Rebel Slave Communities in the Americas*, pp. 230–245. Richard Price (Ed.). Garden City: Anchor Press.
Eisner, Gisela
1961 *Jamaica, 1830–1930: A Study in Economic Growth.* Manchester: The University Press.
Elder, J.D.
1968 The Male/Female Conflict in Calypso. *Caribbean Quarterly.* 14(3):23–41.
Emecheta, Buchi
1976 *The Bride Price.* New York: George Braziller.
Espeut, Peter
1997 Emancipation: The Legal Process. *The Daily Gleaner.* (August 6):A4.
Ethiopia Africa Black International Congress Church of Salvation
n.d. *Newsletter, Mimeograph.* 10 Miles, Bull Bay, Jamaica.
The Europa World Year Book.
1995 Jamaica. Vol 1. Europa Publications, Ltd.

Faith, Karlene
    1990 One Love—One Heart—One Destiny. A Report on the
    Rastafarian Movement in Jamaica. In *Cargo Cults and
    Millenarian Movements: Transoceanic Comparisons of New
    Religious Movements,* pp. 295–342. G.W. Trompf (Ed.). Berlin:
    Mouton de Gruyter.
Faithhorn, Elizabeth
    1975 The Concept of Pollution among the Kafe of the Papua New
    Guinea Highlands. In *Toward an Anthropology of Women,* pp.
    127–140. Rayna Reiter (Ed.). New York: Monthly Review Press.
Fanon, Frantz
    1968 *The Wretched of the Earth.* New York: Grove Press, Inc.
Farr, T.
    1993 Drug-producing Plants. From Use to Abuse. *Jamaica
    Journal.* 24(3):62–63.
Ferdinand, Dinnys Luciano
    1996 Marginalisation and Gay Families in Latin America and the
    Caribbean. *Gender and Development.* 4(2):47–51.
Ford-Smith, Honor
    1997 Ring Ding in a Tight Corner: Sistren, Collective Democracy,
    and the Organization of Cultural Production. In *Feminist
    Genealogies, Colonial Legacies, Democratic Futures,* pp.
    213–258. M. Jacqui Alexander and Chandra T. Mohanty (Eds.).
    New York: Routledge.
Forsythe, Dennis
    1983 *Rastafari: For the Healing of the Nation.* Kingston: Zaika
    Publications.
French, Joan and Ann-Marie Bonner
    1989 *No. To Sexual Violence.* Kingston: Sistren Research.
French, Joan
    1988 Colonial Policy Towards Women after the 1938 Uprising:
    The Case of Jamaica. *Caribbean Quarterly.* 34(1–2):38–61.
French, Joan and H. Ford-Smith
    1986 Women and Organization in Jamaica 1900–1944.
    Unpublished Research. Women and Development Studies, Institute
    of Social and Economic Research. The Hague, Holland.
Garcia, Alma
    1989 The Development of Chicana Feminist Discourse,
    1970–1980. *Gender and Society.* 3(2):217–238.

Garofalo, Reebee
    1987 How Autonomous is Relative: Popular Music, the Social
    Formation and Cultural Struggle. *Popular Music*. 6(1):77–92.
Garvey, Amy Jacques
    1967 *Philosophy and Opinions of Marcus Garvey*. New York:
    Antheneum.

_____
    1978 *Garvey and Garveyism*. New York: Octagon Books.
Gaspar, Barry and Darlene Hine
    1996 *Black Women and Slavery in the Americas. More Than
    Chattel*. Bloomington: Indiana University Press.
Genovese, Eugene D.
    1981 *From Rebellion to Revolution: Afro-American Slave Revolts
    in the Making of the Modern World*. New York: Vintage Books.
Giddings, Paula.
    1992 The Last Taboo. In *Race-ing Justice, En-gendering Power:
    Essays on Anita Hill, Clarence Thomas and the Construction of
    Social Reality*. Toni Morrison (Ed.). New York: Pantheon Books.
Gilroy, Paul.
    1991 *There Ain't No Black in the Union Jack: The Cultural
    Politics of Race and Nation*. Chicago: University of Chicago Press.
Girvan, Norman, and Owen Jefferson (Eds.)
    1971 *Readings in the Political Economy of the Caribbean*.
    Kingston: New World Group.
Gjerset, Heidi
    1994 First Generation Rastafari in St. Eustatius: A Case Study in
    the Netherlands Antilles. *Caribbean Quarterly*. 40(1):64–77.
Goldenberg, Naomi R.
    1979 *Changing of the Gods: Feminism and the End of
    Traditional Religions*. Boston: Beacon Press.
Gopaul, Lina
    1994 *The Darker Side of Black*. Videorecording. Isaac Julien,
    Writer and Director.
Gordon, Derek
    1996 Women, Work and Social Mobility in Post-War Jamaica. In
    Women and the Sexual Division of Labour in the Caribbean, pp.
    72–86. Keith Hart (Ed.). Mona: Canoe Press, University of the
    West Indies.
Gordon, Lorna
    1986 Silent Crimes against Jamaican Women. In *Women of the
    Caribbean*, pp. 80–83. Pat Ellis (Ed.). London: Zed Books Ltd.

Gordon, Shirley
    1996 *God Almighty Make Me Free*. Bloomington, Indiana:
    Indiana University Press.

Grass, Randall F.
    1984 Reggae in the Promised Land. *The Village Voice*. (March
    6):62.

Gray, Obika
    1991 *Radicalism and Social Change in Jamaica, 1960–1972*.
    Knoxville, Tennessee: The University of Tennessee Press.

Green, William
    1976 *British Slave Emancipation. The Sugar Colonies and the
    Great Experiment, 1830–1865*. Oxford: Clarendon Press.

Grinspoon, Lester
    1995 Marijuana, the AIDS Wasting Syndrome, and the U.S.
    Government. *New England Journal of Medicine*. 333:670–671.

Hafkin, Nancy J. and Edna G. Bay
    1976 *Women in Africa*. Stanford, California: Stanford University
    Press.

Hammond, Evelyn
    1997 Toward a Genealogy of Black Female Sexuality. In *Feminist
    Genealogies, Colonial Legacies, Democratic Futures*, pp.
    170–182. Jacqui M. Alexander and Chandra Mohanty (Eds.).
    New York: Routledge.

Harrison, Faye
    1988 Women in Jamaica's Urban Informal Economy: Insights
    from a Kingston Slum. *Nieuwe West-Indische Gids*.
    62(3–4):103–128.

Hebdige, Dick
    1987 *Cut 'n' Mix. Culture, Identity, and Caribbean Music*. New
    York: Methuen.

Henn, Jeanne
    1986 *The Material Basis of Sexism: A Mode of Production
    Analysis with African Examples*. Working Papers in African
    Studies, No. 119. Boston University: African Studies Center.

Henriques, Fernando
    1952 *Family and Colour in Jamaica*. London: Eyre &
    Spottiswoode.

Henry, Balford
    1993 Mutabaruka: One Angry Man. *Sunday Gleaner*. (June
    20):1D.

Higman, Barry
1984 *Slave Populations of the British Caribbean, 1807–1834.*
Baltimore: Johns Hopkins University Press.

Hill, Robert
1983 Leonard Howell and Millenarian Visions in Early Rastafari.
Jamaica Journal. 16(1):24–39.

Homiak, John P.
1985 The 'Ancients of Days' Seated Black: Eldership, Oral
Tradition and Ritual in Rastafari Culture. PhD Dissertation,
Brandeis University, Waltham, Massachusetts.

hooks, bell
1984 *Feminist Theory: From Margin to Center.* Boston: South
End Press.

Hopkins, Elizabeth
1971 The Nyabinghi Cult of Southwestern Uganda. In *Rebellion
in Black Africa,* pp. 60–132. Robert Rotberg (Ed.). London:
Oxford University Press.

Hyman, Paula
1976 The Other Half: Women in the Jewish Tradition. In *The
Jewish Woman: New Perspectives.* New York: Schocken Books.

Isaacs, Harold
1964 A Name to Go By. In *The New World of Negro Americans,*
pp. 62–71. New York: The Viking Press.

Jones, Angella
1987 Battered Women. *Status of Women in the Caribbean,* pp.
31–37. Report of Regional Seminar Held at Wyndham Hotel,
New Kingston, Jamaica. (December 10–11).

Jones, Lisa
1994 Africa (TM). In *Bulletproof Diva: Tales of Race, Sex, and
Hair,* pp. 298–302. New York: Doubleday.

———
1990 The Signifying Monkees. *Village Voice.* November 6, p.
171.

Jones, Simon
1988 *Black Culture, White Youth: The Reggae Tradition from JA
to UK.* London: Macmillan.

Justus, Joyce Bennett
1981 Women's Role in West Indian Society. In *The Black Woman
Cross-Culturally,* pp. 431–450. Filomena Steady (Ed.).
Cambridge: Schenkman Publishing Company.

Justus, Joyce, Hermione McKenzie, and Dorian Powell
1979 *Increasing Educational and Economic Options of Jamaican Adolescent Females.* New York: Research Institute for the Study of Man.
Kaufman, Michael
1985 *Jamaica Under Manley: Dilemmas of Socialism and Democracy.* Westport: Lawrence Hill.
Kapuscinski, Ryszard
1983 *The Emperor.* New York: Harcourt-Brace-Jovanovich.
Lacey, Terry
1977 *Violence and the Politics in Jamaica, 1960–1970.* Manchester: Manchester University Press.
Lake, Obiagele
n.d. The Dekinking of African Hair—Style or Stigma? (In Progress).

_____ 1994 The Many Voices of Rastafarian Women. *New West Indian Guide.* 68(3–4):235–257.

_____ 1994 Interviews with Rastafarians in Jamaica.

_____ 1985 *Cultural Determinants of Breast Feeding Among Jamaican Rastafarian.* Master's Thesis, Cornell University, Ithaca, New York.

_____ 1993 Interviews with Rastafarian men in Kingston, Jamaica.

_____ 1997 Interviews with Rastafarian men in Kingston and Ocho Rios.
Lamming, George
1970 *In the Castle of My Skin.* New York: MacMillan.
Landman-Bogues, J.
1976 Rastafarian Food Habits. *Cajanus.* 9(4):228–233.
Leacock, Eleanor B.
1981 *Myths of Male Dominance. Collected Articles on Women Cross-Culturally.* New York: Monthly Review Press.
LeFranc, Elsie
1988 Higglering in Kingston: Entrepreneurs or Traditional Small-Scale Operators. *Caribbean Review.* 16(1):18ff.

1996 Petty Trading and Labour Mobility: Higglers in the
Kingston Metropolitan Area. In *Women and the Sexual Division
of Labour in the Caribbean,* pp. 103–131. Keith Hart (Ed.).
Mona: Canoe Press, University of the West Indies.

Lehrman, Sally
1995 U.S. Stalls over Tests of Marijuana to Treat AIDS. *Nature.*
374:7–8.

LeMoyne, James
1990 The Men Who Took Aim at Rap Groups. *New York Times.*
(June 12).

Leo-Ryhnie, Elsa
1987 The Role of Women in Caribbean Society. *Status of Women
in the Caribbean,* pp. 20–27. Report of Regional Seminar Held at
Wyndham Hotel, New Kingston, Jamaica. (December 10–11).

Levitt, Kari Polany
1991 *The Origins and Consequences of Jamaica's Debt Crisis.
1970–1990.* Mona: Consortium Graduate School of Social Sciences.

Lewis, Kingsley
1985 *The Moravian Mission in Barbados, 1816–1886.* Frankfurt:
Verlag Peter Lang.

Lewis, Maureen Warner
1994 *Garvey: Africa, Europe, the Americas.* Trenton: African
World Press, Inc.

Lewis, Rupert
1988 *Marcus Garvey: Anti-Colonial Champion.* Trenton: African
World Press, Inc.

Lewis, William
1993 *Soul Rebels. The Rastafari.* Prospect Heights: Waveland
Press, Inc.

Li, Hui-Lin
1975 The Origin and Use of Cannabis in Eastern Asia: Their
Linguistic-Cultural Implications. In *Cannabis and Culture,* pp.
51–62. Vera Rubin (Ed.). The Hague: Mouton.

Lieb, Elliott and Renee Romano
1983 *Rastafari. 1983 Conversations Concerning Women.* Video
Project.

Lindsay, Beverly
1980 *Comparative Perspectives of Third World Women. The
Impact of Race, Sex, and Class.* New York: Praeger Publishers.

Llaloo, Sister
    1981 Rastawoman as Equal. *Yard Roots*. 1(1):7.
Lobdell, Richard A.
    1988 Women in the Jamaican Labor Force, 1881–1921. *Social and Economic Studies*. 37(1–2):203–240.
Long, Edward
    1970 (1774) *The History of Jamaica*. London: Frank Cass.
Lorde, Audre
    1986 Is Your Hair Still Political? *Essence*. (September) 21:40.
MacCormack, Carol P.
    1985 Lay Concepts Affecting Utilization of Family Planning Services In Jamaica. *Journal of Tropical Medicine and Hygiene*. 88:281–285.
Macleod, Arlene
    1991 *Accommodating Protest. Working Women, the New Veiling, and Change in Cairo*. New York: Columbia University Press.
Mama, Amina
    1996 *The Hidden Struggle. Statutory and Voluntary Sector Responses to Violence against Black Women at Home*. London: Whiting and Birch, Ltd.
Mansingh, Ajai and Laxmi Mansingh
    1985 Hindu Influences on Rastafarianism. *Caribbean Quarterly*. Monograph, pp. 96–115.
Martin, Tony
    1983 *The Pan-African Connection: From Slavery to Garvey and Beyond*. Dover: New Marcus Garvey Library.

——
    1976 *Race First. Ideology and Organizational Struggles of Marcus Garvey and the Universal Negro Improvement Association*. Westport: Greenwood Press.
Mathurin (Mair), Lucille
    1975 *The Rebel Woman in the British West Indies During Slavery*. Kingston: Institute of Jamaica.
Mbilinyi, Marjorie
    1989 Women as Peasants and Casual Labor and the Development Crisis in Tanzania. In *Women and Development in Africa. Comparative Perspectives*, pp. 209–256. Jane Parpart (Ed.). Lanham, Maryland: University Press of America, Inc.

McAfee, Kathy.
1991 *Storm Signals. Structural Adjustment and Development Alternatives in the Caribbean.* Boston: South End Press.

McClendon, Thomas
1995 Tradition and Domestic Struggle in the Courtroom: Customary Law and the Control of Women in Segregation-Era Natal. *The International Journal of African Historical Studies.* 28(3):527–561.

Meigs, Anna S.
1991 *Food Sex and Pollution. A New Guinea Religion.* New Brunswick: Rutgers University Press.

Mitchell, Faith M.
1983 Popular Medical Concepts in Jamaica and their Impact on Drug Use. *Western Journal of Medicine.* 139(6):841–847.

Mohammed, Patricia
1994 Nuancing the Feminist Discourse in the Caribbean. *Social and Economic Studies.* 43(3):137–167.

_____
1997 A Blueprint for Gender in Creole Trinidad: Exploring Gender Mythology through Calypsos of the 1920's and 1930's. Paper presented at Caribbean Studies Association Conference, Barranquilla, Colombia.

Moore, Henrietta
1988 *Anthropology and Feminism.* Cambridge, United Kingdom: Polity Press.

Morrish, Ivor
1982 *Obeah, Christ and Rastaman: Jamaica and its Religion.* Cambridge: James Clarke.

Mosley, Leonard
1964 *Haile Selassie: The Conquering Lion.* Englewood Cliffs: Prentice-Hall Inc.

Moyne Commission Report (MCR)
1938 Report of the West India Royal Commission appointed 5th August 1938.

Munroe, Trevor
1972 *The Politics of Constitutional Decolonization: Jamaica 1944–62.* Mona: Institute of Social and Economic Research, University of West Indies.

Narasimhan, Sakuntala
1990 *Sati. Widow Burning in India.* New York: Doubleday.

National Report on the Status of Women in Jamaica
1995 Prepared for the Fourth World Conference on Women, Beijing, China. Kingston: The Jamaican National Preparatory Commission.

Nettleford, Rex
1970 *Mirror, Mirror: Identity, Race, and Protest in Jamaica.* Kingston: William Collins and Sangsters.

_____ 1974 African Redemption. The Rastafari and the Wider Society, 1959–1969. In *Mirror, Mirror, Identity: Race and Protest in Jamaica,* pp. 39–112. London: William Collins and Sangster (Jamaica) Ltd.

Newsweek
1980 Jamaica: Back in Business. (December 15) 96:86.

Nicholas, Tracy
1979 *Rastafari. A Way of Life.* New York: Anchor Books.

Obbo, Christine
1980 *African Women. Their Struggle for Economic Independence.* London: Zed Press.

Owens, Joseph
1976 *Dread. The Rastafarians of Jamaica.* Jamaica: Montrose Printery, Ltd.

Pankhurst, Alula
1992 *Resettlement and Famine in Ethiopia: The Villager's Experience.* Manchester: Manchester University Press.

Panton, David
1993 Dual Labor Markets and Unemployment in Jamaica: A Modern Synthesis. *Social and Economic Studies.* 42(1):75–118.

Parpart, Jane
1995 *Gender, Patriarchy and Development in Africa: The Zimbabwean Case.* East Lansing: Women in International Development, Michigan State University.

Patterson, Orlando
1982 *Slavery and Social Death: A Comparative Study.* Cambridge: Harvard University Press.

_____ 1973 Slavery and Slave Revolts: A Sociohistorical Analysis of the First Maroon War 1665–1740. In *Maroon Societies: Rebel Slave Communities in the Americas,* pp. 246–292. Richard Price (Ed.). Garden City: Anchor Books.

Patterson, Sheila
1963 *Dark Strangers*. London: Tavistock.
Perkins, William Eric
1996 The Rap Attack. In *Dropping Science: Critical Essays on Rap Music and Hip Hop Culture*. pp. 1–48. Philadelphia: Temple University Press.
Petras, Elizabeth M.
1988 *Labor Migration in Jamaica: White Capital and Black Labor, 1850–1930*. Boulder: Westview Press.
Phillips, Hilary
1987 *Status of Women in the Caribbean*, pp. 38–59. Report of Regional Seminar held at Wyndham Hotel, New Kingston, Jamaica. (December 10–11).
Pollard, Velma
1994 *Dread Talk. The Language of Rastafari*. Kingston: Canoe Press University of the West Indies.
Population Census
1991 *Jamaica*. Kingston: Statistical Institute of Jamaica.
Population Census
1982 *Jamaica*. Kingston: Statistical Institute of Jamaica.
Post, Ken
1978 *Arise Ye Starvelings: The Jamaican Labour Rebellion of 1938 and Its Aftermath*. The Hague: Martinus Nijoff.
Powell, Dorian
1986 Caribbean Women and Their Response to Familial Experience. *Social and Economic Studies*. 35(2):83–180.
Quevedo, Raymond (Atilla the Hun)
1983 *Atilla's Kaiso. A Short History of Trinidad Calypso*. St. Augustine: University of the West Indies.
Quiñones-Perdomo, Joann
1997 Personal Communication.
Raming, Ida
1976 *The Exclusion of Women from the Priesthood*. Metuchen: The Scarecrow Press.
Randall, R.C.
1990 *Cancer Treatment and Marijuana Therapy*. Washington, D.C.: Galen Press.
Ray, Ella
1997 *Standing in the Lion's Shadow: Jamaican Women and the Changing Gender Roles in Rastafari*. Dissertation, John Hopkins University, Baltimore, Maryland.

Reckford, Verena
1977 Rastafarian Music: An Introductory Study. *Jamaica Journal.*
(August 30), 11(1–2):3–13.

Reddock, Elizabeth Rhoda
1984 *Women, Labour and Struggle in 20th Century Trinidad and
Tobago: 1896–1960.* Amsterdam: Universiteit van Amsterdam.

Renzetti, Claire and Daniel J. Curran
1989 *Women, Men and Society. The Sociology of Gender.* Boston:
Allyn and Bacon.

Richardson, Mary F.
1983 Out of Many, One People—Aspiration or Reality? An
Examination of the Attitudes to the Various Racial and Ethnic
Groups within the Jamaican Society. *Social and Economic Studies.*
32(3):143–167.

Robertson, Diane
1982 *Jamaican Herbs. Nutritional and Medicinal Values.*
Kingston: Jamaican Herbs Limited.

Rodney, Walter
1990 *The Groundings with My Brothers.* Chicago: Research
Associates School Times Publications.

——— 1972 *How Europe Underdeveloped Africa.* London: Bogle-
L'Ouverture Publications.

Rodriguez, Jeanette
1994 *Our Lady of Guadalupe. Faith and Empowerment among
Mexican-American Women.* Austin: University of Texas.

Rosaldo, Renato
1989 *Culture and Truth: The Remaking of Social Analysis.*
Boston: Beacon Press.

Rosaldo, Michelle and Louise Lamphere
1974 *Women, Culture and Society.* Stanford: Stanford University
Press.

Ross-Frankson, Joan and Cheryl Fletcher
n.d. A Crime against Children. *Sistren.* 12(2–3):20–21.

Rounder Records Corporation
1990 *Calypso Breakaway. 1927–1941.* Cambridge: Rounder
Records Corp.

Rowe, Maureen
1985 The Woman in RastafarI. *Caribbean Quarterly.*
Monograph, pp. 13–21. University of West Indies: United Cooperative Printers, Ltd.

Rubin, Gayle
1975 The Traffic in Women: Notes on the 'Political Economy' of Sex. In *Toward an Anthropology of Women*, pp. 157–210. Rayna R. Reiter (Ed.). New York: Monthly Review Press.
Rubin, Vera and Lambros Comitas
1988 *Ganja in Jamaica*. The Hague: Mouton Press.
Ruether, Rosemary Radford
1974 *Religion and Sexism. Images of Women in the Jewish and Christian Traditions*. New York: Simon and Schuster.
Rushing, Andrea Benton
1988 Hair Raising. *Feminist Studies*. 14(2):325–335.
Russell, Diana E. H.
1992 *A Selected Bibliography on Male Violence Against Women and Girls in South Africa*. Cape Town: Institute of Criminology, University of Cape Town.
Russell, Kathy, Midge Wilson and Ronald Hall
1992 *The Color Complex. The Politics of Skin Color Among African Americans*. New York: Harcourt-Brace-Jovanovich.
Safa, Helen
1986 Economic Autonomy and Sexual Equality in Caribbean Society. *Social and Economic Studies. Special Issue: Women in the Caribbean*. (June, Part 2) 35:2.
Savishinsky, Neil
1994 Rastafari in the Promised Land: The Spread of a Jamaican Socioreligious Movement among the Youth of West Africa. *African Studies Review*. (December) 37(3):19– 50.
Scott, Matthew S. and Nicole Lewis
1992 Growth for Jamaica? *Black Enterprise*. (December) 23:22.
Seaga, Edward
1982 *Revival Cults in Jamaica: Notes Towards a Sociology of Religion*. Kingston: The Institute of Jamaica.
Segal, Ronald
1995 *The Black Diaspora*. New York: Farrar, Straus and Giroux.
Semaj, Leachim
1985 Rastafari: From Religion to Social Theory. *Caribbean Quarterly*, pp. 22–31. Monograph. Kingston, Jamaica: University of the West Indies.
Sen, G. and C. Grown
1987 *Development, Crisis, and Alternative Visions. Third World Women's Perspectives*. New York: Monthly Review Press.

Senior, Olive
    1991 *Working Miracles. Women's Lives in the English-Speaking Caribbean.* Cave Hill: Institute of Social and Economic Research, University of the West Indies.

Sheridan, Richard
    1989 Changing Sugar Technology and the Labor Nexus in the British Caribbean, 1750–1900, with Special Reference to Barbados and Jamaica. *New West Indian Guide.* 63(1–2):59–93.

——— 1985 *Doctors and Slaves: A Medical and Demographic History of Slavery in the British West Indies, 1680–1834.* Cambridge: Cambridge University Press.

Sigot, Asenath, Lori Ann Thrupp, and Jennifer Green
    1995 *Towards Common Ground. Gender and Natural Resource Management in Africa.* Washington, D.C.: World Resources Institute.

Silvera, Makeda Patricia
    1992 *Piece of My Heart. A Lesbian of Colour Anthology.* Canada: Sister Vision. Black Women and Women of Colour Press.

Simpson, George
    1985 Religion and Justice: Some Reflections on the Rastafari Movement. *Phylon.* 46(4):286–291.

——— 1956 Jamaican Revivalist Cults. *Social and Economic Studies.* 5:321–442.

Simpson, Portia
    1997 We Can Stand with Pride in the World. *The Daily Gleaner.* (August 14):B5.

Singer, Beverly R.
    1992 American Indian Women Killing: A Tewa Native Woman's Perspective In *Femicide, The Politics of Woman Killing,* pp. 170–176. Jill Radford and Diana Russell (Eds.). New York: Twayne Publishers.

Smith, Barbara
    1995 Negotiating Difference-Black Nations/Queer Nations. *Gay Community News.* 21(2):4, 10, 20–22, 29.

Smith, M.G., Roy Augier, and Rex Nettleford.
    1960 *The Rastafari Movement in Kingston, Jamaica.* Kingston: Institute of Social and Economic Research.

Sorenson, John
    1992 Essence and Contingency in the Construction of
    Nationhood: Transformation of Identity in Ethiopia and its
    Diasporas. *Diaspora.* 2(2):201–228.
Spaulding, Gary
    1993 MP Blasts Status of JA Women. *The Daily Gleaner.* (July 15).
Standing, Guy
    1981 *Unemployment and Female Labour.* New York: St. Martin's
    Press.
Stapleton, Chris and Chris May
    1987 *African All-Stars: The Pop Music of a Continent.* London:
    Paladin Grafton Books.
Statistical Institute of Jamaica
    1982 *Population Census (Final Count).* Kingston: STATIN.
Steady, Filomena Chioma
    1987 African Feminism: A Worldwide Perspective. In *Women in
    Africa and the African Diaspora,* pp. 3–24. Rosalyn Terborg-Penn,
    Sharon Harley, and Andrea Rushing (Eds.). Washington, D.C.:
    Howard University Press.
Steel Pulse
    1986 *Babylon the Bandit.* Electra.
Stewart, Robert J.
    1992 *Religion and Society in Post—Emancipation Jamaica.*
    Knoxville: University of Tennessee Press.
Stone, Carl
    1991 Hard Drug Use in a Black Island Society—A Survey of Drug
    Use in Jamaica. *Caribbean Studies.* 24(3–4):267–288.

——   1975 Bauxite and National Development in Jamaica. A paper
    delivered at the Symposium on International Aspects of the
    Bauxite Industry, University of West Indies, Mona. (May 17).
    [Mimeographed.]
Sudarkasa, Niara
    1987 "The Status of Women" in Indigenous African Societies.
    Women in Africa and the African Diaspora, pp. 25–42. Rosalyn
    Terborg-Penn, Sharon Harley and Andrea Benton Rushing (Eds.).
    Washington, D.C.: Howard University Press.
Swantz, L.W.
    1965 The Zamaro of Tanzania. Dar es Salaam: Nordic Project
    Tanganyika. [Mimeographed.]

Tareke, Gebru
    1991 *Ethiopia: Power and Protest. Peasant Revolts in the Twentieth Century.* Cambridge: Cambridge University Press.
Tarte-Booth, Christine
    1984 400 Years: A History of Cultural Resistance in Jamaica. Thesis, The University of Minnesota.
Taylor, Timothy
    1984 Soul Rebels: The Rastafarians and the Free Exercise Clause. *Georgetown Law Journal.* 72:1605–1635.
Terborg-Penn, Rosalyn, Sharon Harley and Andrea B. Rushing
    1987 *Women in Africa and the African Diaspora.* Washington, D.C.: Howard University Press.
Terrelonge, Pauline.
    1995 Femininist Consciousness and Black Women. In *Words of Fire: An Anthology of African-American Feminist Thought,* pp. 490–501. Beverly Guy-Sheftall (Ed.). New York: The New Press.
Tomlinson, John.
    1991. *Culturalism Imperialism.* Baltimore: Johns Hopkins University Press.
Tramm, Madeleine L.
    1977 Multinationals in Third World Development: The Case of Jamaica's Bauxite Industry. *Caribbean Quarterly.* 23(4):1–16.
Trepper, Beth
    1984 Skanking with the Supai. *Reggae and African Beat.* (April) 3(2):13–15, 45.
Turner, Mary
    1982 *Slaves and Missionaries: The Disintegration of Jamaican Slave Society, 1987–1834.* Urbana: University of Illinois Press.
Turner, Terisa
    1991 Women, Rastafari and the New Society: Caribbean and East African Roots of a Popular Movement against Structural Adjustment. *Labour, Capital and Society.* 24(1):66–89.
Turner, Jonathan, Royce Singleton, Jr, and David Musick
    1984 *Oppression: A History of Black-White Relations in America.* Chicago: Nelson-Hall.
Ullrich, H. E.
    1992 Menstrual Taboos among Hvik Brahmin Women: A Study of Ritual Change. *Sex Roles: A Journal of Research.* (January) 26(1–2):19–40.

U.S. Department of Labor
  1965 *The Negro Framily: The Case for National Action.* (The Moynihan Report.) Washington, D.C.: U.S. Government Printing Office.

Uta, Ranke-Heinemann
  1990 *Eunuchs for Heaven: The Catholic Church and Sexuality.* London: A. Deutsch.

van Dijk, Frank Jan
  1988 The Twelve Tribes of Israel: Rasta and the Middle Class. *New West Indian Guide.* 62(1–2):1–26.

Vergne, Teresita Martinez
  1994 The Liberation of Women in the Caribbean: Research Perspectives for the Study of Gender Relations in the Post-Emancipation Period. *Caribbean Studies.* (January–June) 27(1–2):1–36.

Walker, Alice
  1983 *In Search of Our Mothers' Gardens: Womanist Prose.* San Diego: Harcourt-Brace-Jovanovich.

Walker, Alice and Pratibha Parmar
  1993 *Warrior Marks. Female Genital Mutilation and the Sexual Blinding of Women.* London: Jonathan Cape.

Walters, Basil
  1997 Emancipation, Reparation and Spanish Town. *The Daily Observer.* (August 11):7.

Warner, Keith Q.
  1988 Calypso, Reggae, and Rastafarianism. *Popular Music and Society.* 12:1, 61.

Waters, Anita M.
  1985 *Race, Class, and Political Symbols. Rastafari and Reggae in Jamaican Politics.* New Brunswick: Transaction Books.

Watson, Llewellyn
  1973 Social Structures and Social Movements: The Black Muslims and the Rastafarians in Jamaica. *British Journal of Sociology.* 24(2):188–198.

Webber, J.
  1983 Between Law and Custom: Women's Experience of Judaism. In *Women's Religious Experience: Cross-Cultural Perspectives,* pp. 143–162. P. Holden (Ed.). London: Croom Helm.

West, Cornel
  1994 Commentary in *The Darker Side of Black.* Videorecording. Lina Gopaul (Director).

West, M.E. and A.B. Lockhart
1978 The Treatment of Glaucoma Using a Non-Psychoactive
Preparation of Cannabis Sativa. *West Indian Medical Journal*. 27.

White, Shane and Graham White
1995 Slave Hair and African American Culture in the Eighteenth
and Nineteenth Centuries. *The Journal of Southern History*.
(February), 41(1):45–76.

White, Timothy
1984 *Catch a Fire. The Life of Bob Marley*. London: Corgi
Books.

Whittaker, Lurline
1980 The Impact of Female Education and Other Selected
Variables. Ph.D. Dissertation, Pennsylvania State University.

Williams, Eric
1961 *Capitalism and Slavery*. New York: Russell and Russell.

Williams, K. M.
1981 *The Rastafarians*. London: Ward Lock Educational.

_____ 1986 The Rastafari: Millennial Cultists or Unregenerate Peasants?
Peasant Studies. 14(1):6–26.

Williamson, John
1817 *Medical and Miscellaneous Observation, Relative to the
West Indian Islands*. Vol. 1. Edinburgh, England.

Wilmot, Swithin
1995 "Females of Abandoned Character"? Women and Protest in
Jamaica, 1838–1865. In *Engendering History: Caribbean Women
in Historical Perspective*, pp. 279–295. Verene Shepherd, Bridget
Brereton, and Barbara Bailey (Eds.). New York: St. Martin's Press.

Winger, G., F.G. Hofmann, and J.H. Woods
1992 *A Handbook on Drug and Alcohol Abuse: The Biomedical
Aspects*. New York: Oxford University Press.

Yawney, Carol D.
1989 To Grow a Daughter: Cultural Liberation and the Dynamics
of Oppression in Jamaica. In *Feminism: From Pressure to Politics*,
pp. 177–202. A. Milles and G. Finn (Eds.). Montreal: Black Rose
Press.

Authors Index

Subject Index

polygynous marriage system,
100–101
position of women in Africa, 7,
71, 98–102
women's initiation ceremonies, 99
Women, Bedouin, 110–112
Women, Diaspora African, 3–8, 10,
51, 71, 79, 144
Women, Jamaican
1938 Rebellion, 37, 38–41, 43,
82, 178
agricultural labor, 82
and dance hall, 131–133
Biblical teachings, 86
Christianity and violence, 86
class and, 26, 38–39, 41–43,
48–52, 54–55, 73, 164
coalitions, 147
compared with Rasta, 146
contraceptives, 89
economic status, 81–85
education and employment, 53,
88–89
education and women's
family and, 40, 82
fertility, 20, 89
hair, 146
Higgling (Informal Commercial
Traders), 84
incest, 92
inferiority, 86
Informal Sector, 56–57, 83–84,
161

Jamaican Women's Federation, 40
male violence, 64, 79, 87, 89–92,
119, 142, 180
media, 3, 12, 79, 86–87, 136–137
men as heads of household,
87–88, 146
Moyne Report, 41, 176
compared to Moyne
Commission report, 41
Moynihan Report, 41, 184
mythical Jamaican matriarchy, 84
patriarchy, 40, 147–148, 177
political marginaliztion, 79
positions in the government,
79–82
post 1938 Rebellion, 38–41, 43
post-emancipation, 26
rape, 20–21, 90–92, 127, 133,
147
sexual abuse, 20, 91, 164
socialization of children, 87
stereotypes, 89
teen-pregnancy, 89
unemployment, 46, 56–57,
82–83, 85, 177, 182
violence against, 12, 75, 86–87,
119, 131, 133–134, 142, 162,
164, 175, 180
wages, 40, 56–57, 82, 85, 89
women's organizations, 10–11, 91

Young Socialist League, 50, 52
